THE

EVERYTHING KIDS'®

LEARNING
SPANISH
BOOK

2ND EDITION

Exercises and puzzles to help you learn *español*

Cecilia I. Sojo

Aadamsmedia

Avon, Massachusetts

PUBLISHER Karen Cooper

DIRECTOR OF ACQUISITIONS AND INNOVATION Paula Munier

MANAGING EDITOR, EVERYTHING® SERIES Lisa Laing

COPY CHIEF Casey Ebert

ACQUISITIONS EDITOR Katrina Schroeder

DEVELOPMENT EDITOR Brett Palana-Shanahan

EDITORIAL ASSISTANT Ross Weisman

EVERYTHING® SERIES COVER DESIGNER Erin Alexander

LAYOUT DESIGNERS Colleen Cunningham, Elisabeth Lariviere, Ashley Vierra, Denise Wallace

An Everything® Series Book.
Everything® and everything.com® are registered trademarks of F+W Media, Inc.

Published by Adams Media, a division of F+W Media, Inc.
57 Littlefield Street, Avon, MA 02322. U.S.A.
www.adamsmedia.com

ISBN 10: 1-4405-0676-0
ISBN 13: 978-1-4405-0676-5
eISBN 10: 1-4405-0677-9
eISBN 13: 978-1-4405-0677-2

Printed by RR Donnelley, Harrisonburg, VA, USA.

20   19   18   17   16   15   14   13

August 2016

This publication is designed to provide accurate and authoritative information with regard to the subject matter covered. It is sold with the understanding that the publisher is not engaged in rendering legal, accounting, or other professional advice. If legal advice or other expert assistance is required, the services of a competent professional person should be sought.
—From a *Declaration of Principles* jointly adopted by a Committee of the American Bar Association and a Committee of Publishers and Associations

Many of the designations used by manufacturers and sellers to distinguish their products are claimed as trademarks. When those designations appear in this book and Adams Media was aware of a trademark claim, the designations have been printed with initial capital letters.

Interior illustrations by Kurt Dolber.
Puzzles by Beth L. Blair.

This book is available at quantity discounts for bulk purchases.
For information, please call 1-800-289-0963.

Library of Congress Cataloging-in-Publication Data
Sojo, Cecilia I.
The everything kids' learning Spanish book. — 2nd ed. / Cecilia I. Sojo.
p. cm. — (An Everything series book)
Revised ed. of: Everything kids' learning Spanish book / Laura K. Lawless.
ISBN-13: 978-1-4405-0676-5 (alk. paper)
ISBN-10: 1-4405-0676-0 (alk. paper)
ISBN-13: 978-1-4405-0677-2 (ebook)
ISBN-10: 1-4405-0677-9 (ebook)
1. Spanish language—Textbooks for foreign—Juvenile literature. 2. Spanish language—Conversation and phrase books—English—Juvenile literature. I. Title. II. Title: Learning Spanish book.
PC4129.E5L386   2010
468.2'421—dc22   2010019549

CONTENTS

INTRODUCTION

Learning Spanish is fun. Do you know why? Because it opens up whole new worlds to you. Spanish is one of the most commonly spoken languages in the world—hundreds of millions of people in dozens of countries speak it. You know Spanish is spoken in Spain, but did you know that it's also spoken in most of Central and South America, from Mexico to Chile? In fact, there are only a few countries in Latin America where Spanish isn't spoken, like Brazil and Belize. There are also millions of Spanish speakers in the United States and in other countries all over the world. So by learning Spanish, you'll be able to talk to all of these people and learn about the similarities and differences between their countries and cultures and your own.

Plus, if you can convince someone like your mom, dad, brother, sister, or best friend to learn Spanish with you, you'll be able to study and practice together. It's a lot more fun learning Spanish when you have someone to speak it with regularly. You can help each other understand the tricky parts and remember what you've learned. Then you'll also have a secret language that only the two of you understand!

Speaking Spanish is useful, too. If you want to travel to other countries, it makes sense to speak the local language. If you visit Argentina or Costa Rica, for example, it will be easier (and more fun!) to eat at restaurants, go shopping, and visit places like zoos and museums when you speak Spanish. Plus, when you go to high school, you have to study a foreign language. If you start learning Spanish now, you'll be ahead of your classmates. Besides that, there are lots of jobs that need Spanish speakers. If you want to be a doctor, a teacher, or a lawyer when you grow up, knowing Spanish will let you talk to many more people than if you just know English. In fact, speaking Spanish will probably make it easier for you to get the job in the first place. And if find out that you like Spanish so much that you want to learn another language, like French or Italian, knowing Spanish will make learning that new language even easier.

The Everything® KIDS' Learning Spanish Book, 2nd Edition will help you start learning Spanish and have fun at the same time. This is a complete introduction to Spanish written especially for kids just like you. Every chapter includes lessons, fun activities, puzzles, and games to help you learn, practice, and have a good time, too. You'll be able to talk about what you love and what you dislike, what you're studying at school, and what you want to do when you grow up. You'll also learn how to count, describe your family and friends, talk about clothes and food, and lots more. And when you've finished the whole book and are ready for more, there is a list of books and websites in the back to help you figure out where to go next. (There's also a glossary to help you remember how to say something in Spanish.)

Speaking Spanish is the first step to getting to know more about different countries, cultures, and people. It's fun to learn and speak, and it's useful too. So let's get started and have fun!

CHAPTER 1

The Basics
Los fundamentos

Alphabet—*Alfabeto*

The Spanish alphabet is similar to the English alphabet, except with one extra letter. Plus, the letters are pronounced differently in Spanish. Here is the Spanish alphabet, including how to say each letter, called *pronunciation,* spelled out for you.

Letter	Example	Pronunciation
A	for *abuelo* (grandfather)	AH
B	for *bueno* (good)	BEH
C	for *cama* (bed)	SEH
D	for *desayuno* (breakfast)	DEH
E	for *edificio* (building)	EH
F	for *falda* (skirt)	EF eh
G	for *gracias* (thank you)	HEH
H	for *hablar* (to talk)	AH cheh
I	for *Italia* (Italy)	EE
J	for *jamón* (ham)	HOH tah
K	for *karate* (karate)	KAH
L	for *leer* (to read)	EL eh
M	for *madre* (mother)	EM eh
N	for *nieve* (snow)	EN eh
Ñ	for *ñame* (yam)	EN yeh
O	for *ocho* (eight)	OH
P	for *pelo* (hair)	PEH
Q	for *queso* (cheese)	KOO
R	for *regalo* (gift)	EHRR eh
S	for *sí* (yes)	ES eh
T	for *tener* (to have)	TEH
U	for *uno* (one)	OO
V	for *ventana* (window)	BEH
W	for *watt* (watt)	DO bleh beh
X	for *rayos X* (X-rays)	EH kees
Y	for *ya* (already)	ee gree EH gah
Z	for *zapato* (shoe)	SEH tah

Alphabet Code

This puzzle looks like it is in code, but you are actually practicing how to sound out the Spanish *alfabeto* (alphabet)! Write the correct letter under each letter sound to find the answer to this riddle:

What kind of insect does well in school?

AH
_A_

ESeh PEH EH ELeh ELeh EE ENeh HEH
_S_ _P_ _E_ _L_ _L_ _I_ _N_ _G_

BEH EH EH
_B_ _e_ _e_

A = AH   L = ELeh

B = BEH   N = ENeh

E = EH   P = PEH

G = HEH   O = OH

I = EE   S = ESeh

UNO. OO, ENeh, OH UNO.

¡Bueno!

3

¡CUIDADO!
Mistake to Avoid

Though they're different in English, the letters *B* and *V* are pronounced exactly the same way in Spanish. The letters are both pronounced "beh," and they make a sound much like the *B* in English. There is no English *V* sound in Spanish.

First sing the alphabet song in English. Easy, right? Now, try singing the alphabet song in Spanish! The new pronunciations and the extra letter might make it tricky, but don't give up. Keep practicing until you can sing the whole song without making a mistake!

Numbers—*Números*

Learning how to count in Spanish is lots of fun and very useful. Once you learn the numbers in Spanish, you can count all kinds of things, like pieces of fruit in the refrigerator, clothes in your closet, or birds in a tree in your backyard. Check out the numbers in the following list:

Number	In Spanish	Pronunciation
0	*cero*	SEH ro
1	*uno*	OO noh
2	*dos*	DOS
3	*tres*	TREHS
4	*cuatro*	KWA tro
5	*cinco*	SEEN ko
6	*seis*	SEHEES
7	*siete*	SEE EH teh
8	*ocho*	O cho
9	*nueve*	NUEH beh
10	*diez*	dee EHS
11	*once*	ON seh
12	*doce*	DO seh
13	*trece*	TREH seh
14	*catorce*	ka TOR seh
15	*quince*	KEEN seh
16	*dieciséis*	dee eh see SEHEES
17	*diecisiete*	dee eh see SEE EH teh

Number	In Spanish	Pronunciation
18	*dieciocho*	dee eh see OH choh
19	*diecinueve*	dee eh see NUEH beh
20	*veinte*	BAIN teh
21	*veintiuno*	bain tee OO noh
22	*veintidós*	bain tee DOHS
23	*veintitrés*	bain tee TRES
24	*veinticuatro*	bain tee KWA troh
25	*veinticinco*	bain tee SEEN koh
26	*veintiséis*	bain tee SEHEES
27	*veintisiete*	bain tee SEE EH teh
28	*veintiocho*	bain tee OH choh
29	*veintinueve*	bain tee NUEH beh
30	*treinta*	TRAIN tah
31	*treinta y uno*	TRAIN tah ee OO noh
32	*treinta y dos*	TRAIN tah ee DOS
40	*cuarenta*	kwa REN tah
41	*cuarenta y uno*	kwa REN tah ee OO noh
42	*cuarenta y dos*	kwa REN tah ee DOHS
50	*cincuenta*	seen KWEN ta
60	*sesenta*	seh SEN tah
70	*setenta*	seh TEN tah
80	*ochenta*	oh CHEN tah
90	*noventa*	noh VEN tah
100	*cien*	SEE EN
1,000	*mil*	MEEL
1,000,000	*un millón*	OON mee YON

Uno, dos, tres...

Jumping Numbers

A frog wants to cross the pond, but he can only jump on lily pads with even numbers. Can you help him find the correct path from *el principio* (the start) to *el fin* (the end)? Hint: The frog can jump straight ahead, left, or right, but not diagonally.

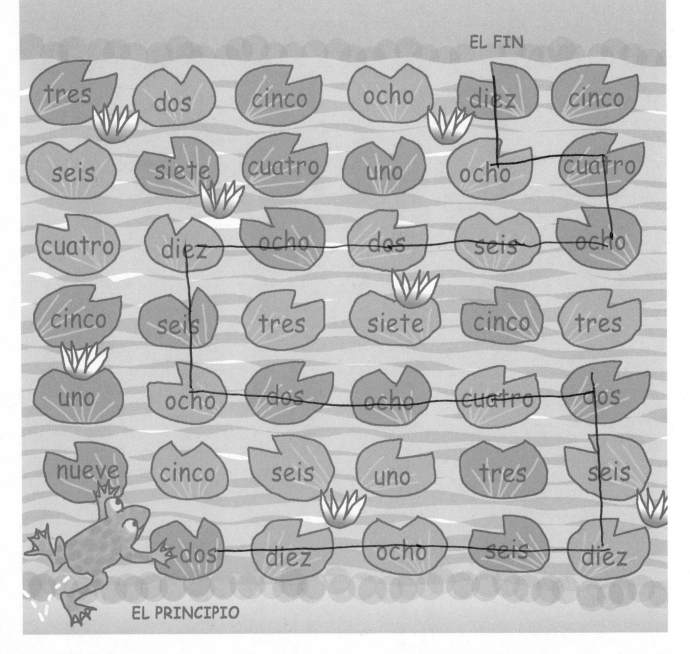

EL FIN

tres	dos	cinco	ocho	diez	cinco
seis	siete	cuatro	uno	ocho	cuatro
cuatro	diez	ocho	dos	seis	ocho
cinco	seis	tres	siete	cinco	tres
uno	ocho	dos	ocho	cuatro	dos
nueve	cinco	seis	uno	tres	seis
dos	diez	ocho	seis	diez

EL PRINCIPIO

To practice using the Spanish numbers, go around your house and count how many of the following items you see. Write your answers in the blank spaces. So, for example, if there are five clocks in your house, your response would look like this:

clocks   _____*cinco*_____

beds   _____

rugs   _____

sinks   _____

televisions   _____

telephones   _____

computers   _____

Gramática — Additional Grammar

When talking about twenties, thirties, and so on, the Spanish numbers are the "tens" word (*veinte, treinta*, etc.) plus the "ones" word (*uno, dos*, etc.) joined by *y* (and). In the twenties, these three words join together in a single word and *y* becomes *i*. For the thirties and up, the three words stay separate. See the list of numbers for more examples.

Nouns—*Nombres*

A noun is a person, place, thing, or idea. For example, here are some nouns in English:

- **Person:** mother, astronaut, Tommy, Mr. Smith
- **Place:** home, space, Chicago, Ireland
- **Thing:** book, suit, city, country
- **Idea:** love, happiness, anger, faith

In Spanish, nouns have what is called "gender," meaning that every noun is either masculine or feminine. When you are talking about people and animals, gender makes sense; some people and animals are masculine (boys, men, lions) and some

la chica

are feminine (girls, women, lionesses). But for other words, gender can seem funny. For example, cheese is masculine (*el queso*) and milk is feminine (*la leche*). But the gender for these nouns does not mean to say cheese is like a boy and milk is like a girl; the gender is just part of the name of each word.

Now, here are some common nouns and their translations in Spanish. Pay attention to the words *el* and *la* that come before each Spanish noun.

English	Spanish	English	Spanish
the father	*el padre*	the mother	*la madre*
the boy	*el chico*	the girl	*la chica*
the cheese	*el queso*	the milk	*la leche*
the love	*el amor*	the happiness	*la felicidad*

He, She, They—*Él, Ella, Ellos, Ellas*

Él and *la* are called "definite articles" and are used when you want to talk about a specific noun. For example, "The book is on the table." You are talking about a specific book and a specific table, so you use the definite articles: *El libro está sobre la mesa.*

Un and *una* are called "indefinite articles" and are used when you are not talking about a specific noun. For example, "Do you have a hat and a scarf?" You are asking whether the person has one of these, so you use the indefinite articles: *¿Tienes un sombrero y una bufanda?*

▼   **ARTICLES FOR MASCULINE NOUNS**

English	Spanish	Pronunciation
the	*el*	Ehl
a	*un*	OOn
some	*unos*	OO nohs

So for example . . .

English	Spanish
the father	*el padre*
a father	*un padre*
some fathers	*unos padres*

▼ **ARTICLES FOR FEMININE NOUNS**

English	Spanish	Pronunciation
the	*la*	Lah
a	*una*	OO nah
some	*unas*	OO nahs

So for example . . .

English	Spanish
the mother	*la madre*
a mother	*una madre*
some mothers	*unas madres*

Verbs—*Verbos*

A verb is an action word: It says what is happening or how something is. Here are some verbs you already know in English:

- to do
- to be
- to go
- to play
- to want
- to hope
- to listen to

¡CUIDADO!
Mistake to Avoid

Here are some words that end in *a* but are masculine: *el clima* (climate), *el día* (day), *el fantasma* (ghost), *el idioma* (language), *el mapa* (map), *el planeta* (planet), *el problema* (problem), *el sofá* (sofa). There are fewer words that end in *o* but are feminine, such as *la mano* (hand).

Consejo
IMPORTANT TIP

There are two words for "you" in Spanish: *tú* is used when you talk to a friend and *usted* is used when you talk to an adult. If you are talking to a group of people, friends and adults alike, you say *ustedes*.

Verbs have many different forms, called "conjugations." Verbs change depending on whether the action is in the present, past, or future, and they also change depending on who is doing the action or being a certain way. For example:

I am going to the store.
You eat a lot.
He walks every day.

The words "I," "you," "he," "she," "we," and "they" are called "subject pronouns." Here are Spanish subject pronouns with their pronunciations:

English	Spanish	Pronunciation
I	yo	YOH
you	tú	TOO
you all	ustedes	ooS TEH dehs
you (formal)	usted	ooS TEHD
you (formal, plural)	ustedes	ooS TEH dehs
he	él	EHL
she	ella	EH ya
we	nosotros	noh SOH tros
they (masculine, mixed gender)	ellos	EH yohs
they (feminine)	ellas	EH yahs

Conjugations are very important. In Spanish, the conjugation is different for every person doing the action, which means that you can actually leave out the subject pronoun, because the verb tells you who is doing the action. For example:

English	Spanish	Spanish (without subject pronoun)
I am going to the store.	Yo voy al mercado.	Voy al mercado.
You are going to the store	Tú vas al mercado.	Vas al mercado.
He is going to the store.	Él va al mercado.	Va al mercado.

Each time you learn a new verb, you have to learn how it is conjugated. But this is not as difficult as it sounds because many verbs follow the same patterns for conjugation. All verbs end in *-ar*, *-er*, or *-ir*, and this ending determines how they will be conjugated. For example, *hablar* (to speak) is an *-ar* verb.

English	Spanish
I speak	*yo hablo*
you speak	*tú hablas*
he speaks	*él habla*

Some other common *-ar* verbs are *amar* (to love), *ayudar* (to help), *lavar* (to wash), and *pagar* (to pay).

Comer (to eat) is an *-er* verb.

English	Spanish
I eat	*yo como*
you eat	*tú comes*
he eats	*él come*

Here are a few more *-er* verbs: *aprender* (to learn), *beber* (to drink), *deber* (to have to), and *leer* (to read).

Abrir (to open) is an *-ir* verb, and *-ir* verbs are conjugated just like *-er* verbs.

English	Spanish
I open	*yo abro*
you open	*tú abres*
he opens	*él abre*

Some useful *-ir* verbs are: *asistir* (to attend), *describir* (to describe), *escribir* (to write), *vivir* (to live).

Some verbs are irregular, which means that they don't follow these conjugation patterns. You'll learn some irregular verbs in this book.

Gramática —
Additional Grammar

The word "it" is usually omitted in Spanish. For example, in the sentence "The book is red," you can replace "the book" with "it": "It is red." In Spanish, The book is red is translated as *El libro es rojo.* To say "It is red," you say, *Es rojo.* Here's another example. In English: "The table is pretty; it is pretty." In Spanish: *La mesa es bonita; Es bonita.*

Pronunciation and Spelling—
Pronunciación y ortografía

Pronunciation means the way that you say a word. Spanish pronunciation is very easy. In fact, it's easier than English pronunciation, because Spanish does not have lots of silent letters and all kinds of different sounds for each vowel. Spanish has one sound for each vowel:

Vowel	Pronunciation
A	"ah" like in "father"
E	"eh" like in "bed"
I	"ee" like in "meek"
O	"oh" like in "go"
U	"oo" like in "moon"

Most of the consonants are very easy too:

Consonant	Pronunciation
B and V	like the "b" in "boy"
D	like the "d" in "do"
F	like the "f" in "father"
K and Q	like the "k" in "kite"
L	like the "l" in "live"
M	like the "m" in "mother"
N	like the "n" in "no"
P	like the "p" in "put"
S and Z	like the "s" in "see"
T	like the "t" in "take"
W (rare in Spanish)	like the "w" in "water"
Y	like the "y" in "yes"

The rest of the Spanish letters are different than the English ones, but with a little practice they are very easy too.

¿Cómo?—
Say What?

Spanish has two other sounds you need to know. The first sound is *ll*. This sound is for words like *llamar* (to call), *calle* (street), and *ella* (she). In some countries people pronounce this letter as "EH jeh" and in some other countries it is pronounced as "EL yay." And *ch* is pronounced like the ch in "cheese." This is found in words like *cheque* (check), *mucho* (a lot), and *muchacho* (boy).

Letter	Pronunciation
H	always silent
Ñ	like the "ni" in "onion"
J	Sound does not exist in English, but the closest sound is like the *h* in "hello."
R	Sound does not exist in English; this is called a "rolled *r*" because it's pronounced by letting your tongue roll against your teeth.
C and G	When *C* is followed by *A*, *O*, *U*, or a consonant, it is pronounced like the *c* in "cat." When *C* is followed by *E* or *I*, it is pronounced like the c in "cell." When *G* is followed by *A*, *O*, *U*, or a consonant, it is pronounced like the *g* in "give." When *G* is followed by *E* or *I*, it is pronounced like the Spanish *J*.
X	Sometimes it is pronounced like the x in "tax." Other times, it is pronounced like the x in "exist."

Hey You!

One kid is talking to an adult teacher, while the other is talking to a cousin the same age. Start at the dot under each word. Follow the maze to find out who is talking to whom!

Consejo
IMPORTANT TIP

The stress in a Spanish word is indicated by an accent mark. The accent means that you should put extra emphasis on that syllable. For example, the Spanish word for pencil is *lápiz*, which is pronounced LA pees. If there is no accent, word stress falls on the last letter of the word. If the word ends in a vowel, *N*, or *S*, the stress is on the second to last syllable: *madre*—MA dreh. If the word ends in anything else, stress is on the last syllable: *calor*—ka LOR.

Pronunciation and spelling are much more closely related in Spanish than in English. The only Spanish letters that cause any real problems with spelling are *H* (because it's silent) and *B* and *V* (because they sound the same). Other than those, what you hear is what you write. Compared to English, with silent letters at the beginning of words (like the *K* in "knife"), in the middle of words (like the *G* in "sign"), and at the end of words (like the *B* in "lamb"), Spanish pronunciation is a piece of cake!

Now that you've learned a little bit about pronunciation, it's time to try speaking some Spanish aloud! Grab a parent or friend and ask if he or she would like to practice with you. Then take turns saying each of the following words aloud. Use the hints if you forget how to pronounce a letter.

Spanish	English	Pronunciation Hint
pollo	chicken	*ll* sounds like the English "y"
verde	green	*v* sounds like "b"
sueño	dream	*ñ* sounds like "ni" in "onion"
queso	cheese	*qu* sounds like the "k" in "kite"
joya	jewel	*j* sounds like the English "h"
hora	hour	*h* is silent

Now that you've had practice saying these words aloud, try having a little conversation with your parent or friend. You can use some of these same words to create a silly conversation using both English and Spanish.

Here's an example:

Jane: Hi, Billy.
Billy: Hello.
Jane: Do you like _____ pollo _____?
Billy: Yes! I especially like it with _____ queso _____.
Jane: Me too. What's your favorite color?
Billy: I really like _____ verde _____.
Jane: Wow! That's the color of the _____ joya _____ in my necklace.

Now use some of these words to write your own silly Spanish-and-English conversation:

Bruce : Hola Judah
Judah: Hola
Bruce: Judah do you like queso?
Judah: Si. I even eat it melted on pollo.
Bruce: What is your favorite color?
Judah: Verde ey azul.
Judah: I like to suneo about verde ailiens.
Bruce: Wow thats the color of my watch.
Judah: Nice seeing you. Adios!
Bruce: Adios!

¡CUIDADO!
Mistake to Avoid

If someone speaks to you and you don't hear him the first time, you may say, "What?" to ask him to repeat himself. In Spanish, you can use *¿qué?* when you are asking a question with "what," like *¿Qué haces?* But when you just want to say "what?" because you didn't hear what someone said, it's more polite to say *¿cómo?*

Questions—*Preguntas*

Just like in English, you can ask "yes or no" questions in Spanish by raising your voice at the end of any sentence. Try it with the following questions:

English	Spanish
Is Miguel ready?	*¿Está listo Miguel?*
Are you thirsty?	*¿Tienes sed?*

Questions that don't have a yes or no answer are a little different. They ask for information, like who, what, when, where, why, and how:

English	Spanish
who	*quién*
what	*qué*
when	*cuándo*
where	*dónde*
why	*por qué*
how	*cómo*
how much	*cuánto*

To ask "who?" feels or is a certain way, just use *quién* plus a verb:

English	Spanish
Who is ready?	*¿Quién está listo?*
Who is thirsty?	*¿Quién tiene sed?*

To ask questions with the other words, use the question word plus the verb. If you want to include the subject pronoun (such as *tú*), put it after the verb:

English	Spanish
What are you doing?	*¿Qué haces? ¿Qué haces tú?*
When are we eating?	*¿Cuándo comemos? ¿Cuándo comemos nosotros?*
Where is Ana?	*¿Dónde está Ana?*

How to Make Questions—*Cómo hacer preguntas*

The most common way to make questions in Spanish is to use words like "When," "How," and "Where," and to begin with an action word. For example:

English	Spanish
Where is the book?	*¿Dónde está el libro?*
Is the book on the table?	*¿Está el libro en la mesa?*
Do you speak with your mother?	*¿Hablas con tu madre?*
When does Maria play in the park?	*¿Cuando juega María en el parque?*

Consejo
IMPORTANT TIP

When you ask a question in Spanish, you need a regular question mark at the end of the question, as well as an upside-down question mark at the beginning. For example, the question "What?" is written *¿Cómo?* And for exclamations, there's an upside-down exclamation point to use at the beginning, like this: *¡Ay, caramba!* (My goodness!) Grab a piece of paper and practice writing these new punctuation marks.

¿Cómo?— Say What?

Expressions like *¿Cómo estás?* and *¿Qué tal?* are good to use when you're talking to a friend. But if you're talking to an adult, you would need to use the formal version: *¿Cómo está usted?* If you are talking to more than one adult, you would say, *¿Cómo están ustedes?*

As you can see, when the question in English starts with "Do" or "Does," you need to use the main verb or action word at the beginning of the sentence.

Here are some common words you are going to use to make and answer questions:

English	Spanish	Pronunciation
yes	*sí*	SEE
no	*no*	NOH
I don't know	*no sé*	no SEH
okay	*de acuerdo*	deh ah KWER doh
who?	*¿quién?*	KEE EN
what?	*¿qué?*	KEH
when?	*¿cuándo?*	KWAN doh
where?	*¿dónde?*	DON deh
why?	*¿por qué?*	por KEH
how?	*¿cómo?*	KOH moh
and	*y*	ee
or	*o*	o

Now try practicing some of these Spanish words by answering the following questions. These are "yes or no" questions, so you can answer with either *sí* or *no*. Write your answers in the blank spaces.

Does your family have a pet? _____

Do you like the color blue? _____

Do you like to read books? _____

Have you ever been to the zoo? _____

Do you enjoy playing sports? _____

Now that you know these words, try putting them into sentences. The following are very useful sentences to use when you need to ask questions or get more information.

English	Spanish	Pronunciation
I have a question.	*Tengo una pregunta.*	TEN goh OO nah preh GOON tah
What does _____ mean?	*¿Qué quiere decir ?*	keh KEE EH reh deh SEER
How do you say _____ in Spanish?	*¿Cómo se dice _____ en español?*	KOH moh seh DEE she _____ en es PAH neeol

If you need someone to repeat something or speak more slowly, you can try these useful phrases:

English	Spanish
What?	*¿Cómo?*
I am sorry, I don't understand.	*Perdón, no comprendo.*
Can you repeat, please?	*¿Puede repetir, por favor?*
Please, more slowly.	*Más despacio, por favor.*
One more time, please.	*Otra vez, por favor.*

Hi, How Are You?—*Hola, ¿cómo estás?*

What's the first thing you say when you greet a friend? Probably, "Hello," right? In English, there are lots of ways to greet people. For example, you can say "Hi," "Hey," or "What's up?" Just like English, Spanish has several different ways to greet people. Here are some common greetings:

Buenas noches.

English	Spanish
Hi, Hello.	*Hola.*
Good morning. Good day.	*Buenos días.*
Good afternoon.	*Buenas tardes.*
Good evening.	*Buenas noches.*

Night and Day

First collect all the dark letters and put them next to the sleepy *niña* (girl). Then collect all the white letters and put them next to the wide-awake *niña*. Use the letters to spell two common Spanish greetings as suggested by the pictures! Write the greetings on the lines provided.

Hint: Don't forget to include the accent on one of the letters!

The Spanish language has all kinds of different ways to ask "how are you?" too.

English	Spanish
How are you?	¿Cómo estás?
How's it going?	¿Qué tal?
What's new?	¿Qué hay de nuevo?
	¿Qué hay de bueno?
	¿Qué cuentas?
	¿Qué es de tu vida?

If someone asks you how you are doing, you can answer with one of the following responses:

English	Spanish
I'm good.	(Estoy) bien.
I'm great.	(Estoy) muy bien.
Nothing (is new).	Nada.
No news.	Sin novedad.
Nothing much.	Nada de particular.
And you?	¿Y tú?
Same here.	Igualmente.
Me too.	Yo también.

Now that you know some basic greetings and responses, why not try a short dialogue? Sit down with a parent or friend and make up a short Spanish conversation. Here's a sample:

EVA: *Hola.*
JORGE: *Buenas tardes.*

EVA: *¿Qué tal?*
JORGE: *Bien. ¿Y tú?*

EVA: *Muy bien, gracias.*

Consejo
IMPORTANT TIP

As mentioned in Chapter 1, using subject pronouns is usually optional. So, if someone asks you *¿Cómo estás?* (How are you?), you can either respond with *Estoy bien* (I am well) or just *Bien* (well).

Me llamo Rosa.

My Name Is . . . — *Me llamo . . .*

When you meet new people, one of the first things you always do is tell each other your names. Here are some common ways to introduce yourself or someone else and learn other people's names in English and Spanish:

English	Spanish
What's your name?	*¿Cómo te llamas?* (informal)
	¿Cómo se llama? (formal)
Who are you?	*¿Quién eres?*
My name is . . .	*Me llamo . . .*
This is . . .	*Éste es . . .*
His name is . . .	*Él se llama . . .*
Her name is . . .	*Ella se llama . . .*
It's nice to meet you.	*Mucho gusto.*

Now fill in the following sentence with your own name:

Me llamo _____.

When you are talking to adults, you probably don't call them by their first names, right? Instead, you use a title plus their last name. For example, you might call your teacher Mr. Smith. Well, it's the same thing in Spanish:

English	Spanish	Spanish abbreviation
Mr.	*Señor*	*Sr.*
Mrs.	*Señora*	*Sra.*
Miss	*Señorita*	*Srta.*
Dr.	*Doctor*	*Dr.*
	Doctora	*Dra.*
Teacher	*Profesor*	*Prof.*
	Profesora	*Profa.*

Diversión—Fun Stuff

Choose a Spanish name to use when you're practicing speaking Spanish. It doesn't have to be one similar to your real name; in fact, sometimes it's more fun to have a name that's completely different! For example, if your real name is Lindsay, you might like to go by Rosa in your Spanish class or when you're practicing Spanish at home.

So, if your neighbor is named Mr. Grant, you would call him *Señor Grant*. If your Spanish teacher is named Mrs. Juárez, you would call her *Profesora Juárez*. It's that easy!

Please and Thank You—*Por favor y gracias*

As you know, it's always important to be polite. It's just the same when you're speaking Spanish, so don't forget the magic words "please" and "thank you."

English	Spanish
please	*por favor*
pretty please	*porfis, por favorcito*
May I . . . ?	*¿Puedo . . . ?*
I want	*Quiero, Deseo*
I would like	*Quisiera*
thank you	*gracias*
thank you very much	*muchas gracias*
Thank you so much!	*¡Cuánto te lo agradezco!*
I appreciate it.	*Te lo agradezco.*
You're welcome.	*De nada.*
Don't mention it.	*No hay de qué.*

If you accidentally bump into someone or do something wrong, the polite thing to do is say you're sorry, right? It's the same in Spanish. The following are some words to use when you need to excuse yourself or apologize:

English	Spanish
pardon me	*perdón, disculpe*
excuse me	*con permiso*
forgive me	*perdóname, discúlpame*
I'm sorry	*lo siento*
I'm very sorry	*lo siento mucho*

Consejo
IMPORTANT TIP

When you ask a question and you're pretty sure that the answer will be yes, you might add "right?" to the end of the sentence. You can also do this in Spanish by putting *¿no?* or *¿verdad?* at the end of the sentence. For example: Miguel is ready, right? *Miguel está listo, ¿verdad?* You're thirsty, right? *Tienes sed, ¿no?*

Hi, Llama!

This *niño* (boy) wants to say a proper "Hi!" to this friendly llama. How does he do it?

Fill in all the boxes with a dot in *el centro* (the center) to find out!

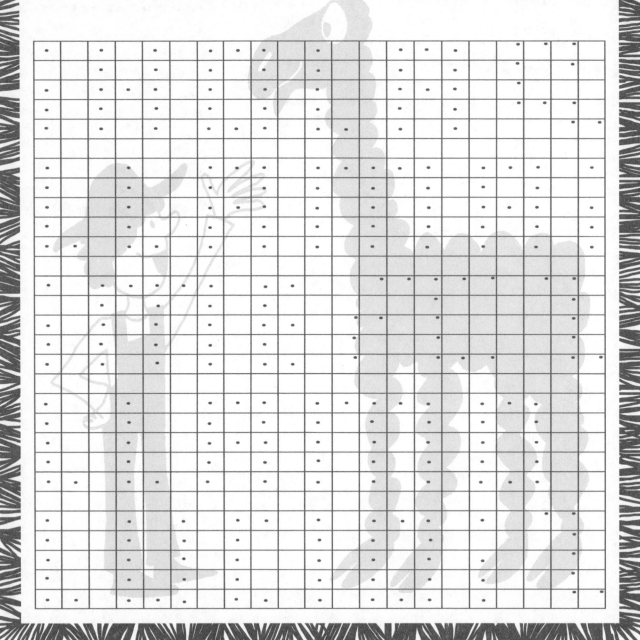

Goodbye—Adiós

Just like there are several ways to greet people in Spanish, there are also various ways to say goodbye. Here are some common phrases to use when you part ways:

English	Spanish
Goodbye.	*Adiós.*
Bye.	*Chao.*
Bye-bye.	*Chaíto.*
See you later.	*Hasta luego.*
	Hasta pronto.
	Hasta la vista.
Catch you later!	*¡Nos vemos!*
See you tomorrow.	*Hasta mañana.*
See you next week.	*Hasta la semana próxima.*
Have a nice day.	*Que tengas un buen día.*
	Que pases un buen día.
Good night.	*Buenas noches.*

> ### ¡CUIDADO!
> **Mistake to Avoid**
>
> *Perdón*, *disculpe*, and *con permiso* are used to be polite, like when you interrupt someone or need someone to move over so that you can get by. *Perdóname* and *discúlpame* are used when you have done something wrong and are asking for forgiveness, like if you broke something or made a mess.

There are also some expressions that are only used for special kinds of goodbyes.

When someone is leaving on a trip, you can say *¡Buen viaje!* (Have a good trip!).

If your friend is taking a test, competing, or doing something else difficult, you can say *¡Buena suerte!* (good luck!) or *¡Que te vaya bien!* (I hope it goes well!).

When saying goodbye to someone they don't expect to see again for a while, some Spanish speakers might say *Que Dios te acompañe* (May God be with you).

Consejo
IMPORTANT TIP

Did you notice the upside-down question marks in the conversation between Jaime and Lupe? They have to be in front of the question, not at the beginning of the line. For example, in the sentence *Nada, ¿y tú?*, "*nada*" is the answer to a question, and then the question "*y tú*" comes after it. So the upside-down question mark goes in front of *y*.

Now that you've read the sample conversations, make up your own! Use Spanish names and as much vocabulary as you can. For example, try one where your friend is leaving on a trip to Spain, and another where your brother or sister is taking a driving test.

Conversations—*Conversaciones*

Now that you know all this new vocabulary, it's time to practice with a friend! Here is a sample conversation to help you get started:

Speaker	English	Spanish
JAIME	Hello.	*Hola.*
LUPE	Hello. What's your name?	*Hola. ¿Cómo te llamas?*
JAIME	My name is Jaime, and you?	*Me llamo Jaime, ¿y tú?*
LUPE	My name is Lupe.	*Me llamo Lupe.*
JAIME	It's nice to meet you.	*Mucho gusto.*
LUPE	Same here.	*Igualmente.*
JAIME	How are you?	*¿Cómo estás?*
LUPE	Fine, and you?	*Bien, ¿y tú?*
JAIME	Same here.	*Igualmente.*
LUPE	Goodbye, Jaime.	*Adiós, Jaime.*
JAIME	Goodbye.	*Adiós.*

CHAPTER 3

People—*La gente*

la abuela

la nieta

My Family—*Mi familia*

Now it's time to talk about family! Since you live with your family, you probably talk with them often and spend lots of time together. Perhaps your parents help you with your homework after school and take you to the park when the weather is nice. This chapter will teach you all you need to know to talk with your family in Spanish!

Every family is different. Some children live with their mother and father, while others only have one parent or live with a relative. The Spanish word for father is *el padre*, and the Spanish word for mother is *la madre*. Or you can call them *Papá* (Dad) and *Mamá* (Mom). Here are the Spanish words for other family members:

English	Spanish	English	Spanish
the grandfather	*el abuelo*	the boy cousin	*el primo*
the grandmother	*la abuela*	the girl cousin	*la prima*
the husband	*el esposo*	the nephew	*el sobrino*
the wife	*la esposa*	the niece	*la sobrina*
the uncle	*el tío*	the son	*el hijo*
the aunt	*la tía*	the daughter	*la hija*
the brother	*el hermano*	the grandson	*el nieto*
the sister	*la hermana*	the granddaughter	*la nieta*

Okay, it's time to practice these new words and see if you can remember what they mean. In the following section you'll be given a Spanish word for a family member. In the blank space, write the name of that person (or one of those people) in your family. So, for example, if you have a cousin named Michael, your response would look like this:

el primo _____Michael_____

Consejo
IMPORTANT TIP

Did you notice that for every one of these family members, the Spanish words for boys and girls are the same except that the boy word ends in *o* and the girl word ends in *a*? When you look at it like that, it's like there are only half as many words to remember. If you know that a boy cousin is *el primo*, then it's easy to remember that a girl cousin is *la prima*.

Now try some on your own. If there is no one in your family with one of these titles, then just leave the space blank.

el tío _____

la abuela _____

la hermana _____

el abuelo _____

la prima _____

el hermano _____

la tía _____

Diversión—Fun Stuff

Use all of your new Spanish vocabulary to make a family tree! To do this, start with yourself and branch out. Write your name and the word *yo*, which means "I" in Spanish. Then draw two lines branching out from you and write your parents' names plus *madre* and *padre*. Keep going until you've included aunts, uncles, cousins, grandparents, and anyone else you can think of! Be sure to show your family tree to your family when you're finished.

When you're talking about your family, there are a few other words you need to know. First is the verb *tener*, which means "to have." *Tengo* means "I have" and *tienes* means "you have." So you can ask your friend *¿Cuántos hermanos y hermanas tienes?* (How many brothers and sisters do you have?) and your friend might answer *Tengo dos hermanos y una hermana.* Now, answer this question about yourself: *¿Cuántos hermanos y hermanas tienes?* Don't forget to write the numbers in Spanish!

Yo tengo _____ *hermanos y* _____ *hermanas.*

The other useful words are "my" and "your." If you're talking about just one family member, you would use *mi* (my) or *tu* (your): *mi padre, mi madre* (my father, my mother), *tu padre, tu madre* (your father, your mother). If you're talking about more than one, you'll use *mis* (my) or *tus* (your): *mis hermanos, mis primos* (my brothers, my cousins), *tus hermanos, tus primos* (your brothers, your cousins).

Now you can talk to and about your family in Spanish! See what you can remember and go practice your new words with a parent or friend.

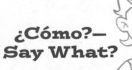

¿Cómo?– Say What?

You might have lots of friends, but you probably only have one best friend. In Spanish, a best friend is *el mejor amigo* or *la mejor amiga.* Here's a question for you: *¿Cómo se llama tu mejor amigo?* (What is your best friend's name?) Remember from Chapter 2 that to answer you can say *Mi mejor amigo (or amiga) se llama . . .* (My best friend's name is . . .).

More People—*Más gente*

Of course, there are lots more people in the world than just the ones in your family. Here are some other Spanish people words you should know:

English	Spanish
a baby boy	*un bebé*
a baby girl	*una bebé*
a boy	*un chico*
	un muchacho
a girl	*una chica*
	una muchacha
a teenage boy	*un joven*
a teenage girl	*una joven*
a man	*un hombre*
a woman	*una mujer*
a boyfriend	*un novio*
a girlfriend	*una novia*

In English, there are a lot of words for people that are the same whether the person is a boy or a girl. But in Spanish, there are two slightly different words for most people. Here are some common people words in English and their Spanish translations:

English	Spanish (male)	Spanish (female)
a neighbor	*un vecino*	*una vecina*
a teacher	*un profesor*	*una profesora*
a student	*un estudiante*	*una estudiante*
a friend	*un amigo*	*una amiga*
my best friend	*mi mejor amigo*	*mi mejor amiga*
a classmate	*un compañero*	*una compañera*
a driver	*un conductor*	*una conductora*
a passenger	*un pasajero*	*una pasajera*

Descriptions and Personality—*Descripciones y personalidad*

Now that you know what to call all of the different people you know, you can describe them. To ask "What is he or she like?" you can say *¿Cómo es?* or *¿Qué tal es?* In English, you might say, "He is tall" or "She is young." Here are some of these answers in Spanish:

English	Spanish	English	Spanish
I am . . .	*Yo soy . . .*	thin	*delgado*
He is . . .	*Él es . . .*	young	*joven*
She is . . .	*Ella es . . .*	old	*viejo*
tall	*alto*	good-looking	*guapo*
short	*bajo*	ugly	*feo*
fat	*gordo*		

bajo   alto

For example, *Él es bajo y delgado* means "He is short and thin." But what if you're describing a girl? In this case, you might need to change the ending of the word from *o* to *a*. For example, a tall girl is *alta*, and a pretty girl is *guapa*. The only word in this list that this doesn't work for is *joven*, which remains the same for a boy or a girl.

Now try describing yourself! For example:

I am young.   ___Yo soy joven.___

Fill in the blanks to complete a sentence describing yourself:

Yo soy _____ *y* _____ .

In English, the adjective (the describing word) comes before the noun; but it's the opposite in Spanish. When you speak Spanish, be sure to say the adjective after the noun.

Gramática — Additional Grammar

If you're describing a girl, you would start with *Ella es* and then change the *o* at the end of the describing word to *a*: *Ella es alta* (she is tall), *ella es guapa* (she is pretty). If you're describing yourself, you would say *yo soy* and then the describing word ending with *o* if you're a boy and *a* if you're a girl. For example, *Yo soy bajo* (I'm short, for a boy) or *Yo soy guapa* (I'm pretty, for a girl).

So, for example, if a person has blue eyes, you would say she has *ojos azules* (eyes blue). To form a complete sentence, start with *él tiene* (he has) or *ella tiene* (she has), then *ojos* (eyes), then the color. Here are some examples:

English	Spanish
He has blue eyes.	*Él tiene ojos azules.*
She has green eyes.	*Ella tiene ojos verdes.*
Juan has gray eyes.	*Juan tiene ojos grises.*
Ana has brown eyes.	*Ana tiene ojos castaños.*

When you talk about someone's hair, it's just the same: *él tiene* or *ella tiene*, plus *cabello* or *pelo* (hair), and then the color or other description word. The words *pelo* and *cabello* both mean hair, so you can use whichever one you want. Here are some hair descriptions you can use:

English	Spanish
dark hair	*cabello/pelo oscuro*
black hair	*cabello/pelo negro*
brown hair	*cabello/pelo castaño*
red hair	*cabello/pelo rojo*
blond hair	*cabello/pelo rubio*
straight hair	*cabello/pelo liso*
curly hair	*cabello/pelo rizado*
wavy hair	*cabello/pelo ondulado*
short hair	*cabello/pelo corto*
long hair	*cabello/pelo largo*

What type of hair do you have? *Qué tipo de pelo tienes?* Fill in your answer here:

Yo tengo pelo _____.

Two other words you might want to describe someone are *pecas* (freckles) and *hoyuelos* (dimples). For example:

English	Spanish
He has freckles.	*Él tiene pecas.*
She has dimples.	*Ella tiene hoyuelos.*

←las pecas

Now you know how to describe what everyone looks like, but what about their personality? For these descriptions, you'll use *Él es* or *Ella es*, plus the describing word. For the words that end in *o*, remember to change it to *a* for girls. If it doesn't end in *o*, then it's the same for boys and girls. Here are some adjectives you might use:

English	Spanish	English	Spanish
affectionate	*afectuoso*	outgoing	*extrovertido*
boring	*aburrido*	patient	*paciente*
brave	*valiente*	playful	*juguetón*
friendly	*amistoso*	serious	*serio*
funny	*divertido*	shy	*tímido*
impatient	*impaciente*	smart	*inteligente*
interesting	*interesante*	snobbish	*presumido*
kind	*amable*	strong	*fuerte*
lazy	*perezoso*	studious	*estudioso*
mean	*cruel*	stupid	*estúpido*
nice	*simpático*	weak	*débil*

Do you have an affectionate friend (*un amigo afectuoso*)? An interesting aunt (*una tía interesante*)? Fill in the following blanks to complete sentences describing yourself and your family members. For yourself, you're going to use *Yo soy* again, which means "I am." If you need to, refer back to the beginning of the chapter to review the Spanish words for different family members.

fuerte

Yo soy _____ y _____.

Mi padre es _____ y _____.

Mi madre es _____ y _____.

Mi hermano es _____ y _____.

Mi hermana es. _____ y _____.

Mi abuelo es _____ y _____.

Mi abuela es _____ y _____.

Mi tío es _____ y _____.

Mi tía es _____ y _____.

Mi primo es _____ y _____.

Mi prima es _____ y _____.

Feelings—*Sentimientos*

So now you know how to describe what people look like and what kind of personality they have, but what about how they feel? People's feelings change all the time, so you'll need to learn some new vocabulary to keep up with them.

For most feelings, you'll use the verb *estar* (to be). To say "I am" in Spanish, say *yo estoy*. To say "you are," say *tú eres*. Now, just add one of the following feelings words and you've got yourself a sentence!

English	Spanish
angry	*enojado*
annoyed	*enfadado*
bored	*aburrido*
depressed	*deprimido*

Consejo
IMPORTANT TIP

Remember that to ask how another person feels, you can just make a sentence with the *tú* form of the verb plus the adjective: *¿Estás triste?* (Are you sad?) Or you can use a question word: *¿Por qué estás enojado?* (Why are you angry?) To practice, try having a short conversation with someone in your family. Start by saying hello and asking how he or she feels in Spanish.

English	Spanish
dizzy	*mareado*
embarrassed	*avergonzado*
excited	*entusiasmado*
happy	*feliz, alegre*
jealous	*celoso*
nervous	*inquieto*
offended	*ofendido*
sad	*triste*
sick	*enfermo*
tired	*cansado*

When you feel bored, you can say *Estoy aburrido*. When you feel happy, you can say *Estoy feliz*. These are emotional feelings, which means they describe how your mind feels. For physical feelings (the way your body feels) you can't use *estar*; you need a different verb. This verb is *tener* (to have). In English, you say "I am hungry" or "I am cold," but in Spanish what you literally have to say is *Tengo hambre* (I have hunger) and *Tengo frío* (I have cold). This may seem a little strange because of the way you are used to using "to have" in English. Don't worry; it just takes some getting used to.

To create a sentence using *tener*, start with *yo tengo* (I am) or *tú tienes* (you are). Then, add one of the following:

English	Spanish
hungry	*hambre*
thirsty	*sed*
hot	*calor*
cold	*frío*

To tell someone that you're hungry, you say, *Tengo hambre*. To ask someone if he or she is hot, just ask *¿Tienes calor?* Easy, right? Remember: Practice makes perfect!

¡CUIDADO!
Mistake to Avoid

Even though you should use *estar* with most emotional feeling words (like happy or sad) and *tener* with most physical feeling words (like hot or cold), some words don't follow these rules. For example, to say "I am scared" (an emotional feeling), you would say *Tengo miedo*.

¡Yo tengo frío!

Diversión Fun Stuff

Here's a great way to practice all the Spanish words for body parts: Draw a big picture of a person and label all of the different parts in Spanish. Don't forget all the details, like teeth and fingers. Once you've learned these body part words, you can label them all!

Consejo
IMPORTANT TIP

Did you notice that you use the same word to say both "finger" and "toe" in Spanish? The word *dedo* literally translates as "digit," which is another word you can use for finger and toe in English. If you need to be specific, you can say *dedo del pie*, so that the person you're talking to knows you mean your toe and not your finger. Now that you know how to say finger and toe in Spanish, practice the numbers you learned in Chapter 1 and try counting them: *Un dedo, dos dedos, tres dedos*… How high can you count?

Parts of the Body—*Partes del cuerpo*

Now it's time to learn how to talk about parts of your body. From your head to your toes, it's fun to describe all your parts in Spanish. Here are some good words to know:

English	Spanish
the hair	el cabello, el pelo
the head	la cabeza
the face	la cara
the eye	el ojo
the nose	la nariz
the cheek	la mejilla
the mouth	la boca
the lip	el labio
the tooth	el diente
the ear	la oreja

English	Spanish
the neck	el cuello
the chest	el pecho
the back	la espalda
the stomach	el estómago
the arm	el brazo
the shoulder	el hombro
the elbow	el codo
the wrist	la muñeca
the hand	la mano
the finger	el dedo
the fingernail, the toenail	la uña
the thumb	el pulgar
the leg	la pierna
the knee	la rodilla
the ankle	el tobillo
the foot	el pie
the toe	el dedo del pie

la mano

Face to Face

These *niños* (children) are each missing something! Fill in the blanks with the correct English word and complete each picture.

I see ____ my _____.
Yo veo <u>con</u> mis <u>ojos</u>.

I smell ____ my _____.
Yo huelo <u>con</u> mi <u>nariz</u>.

I hear ____ my _____.
Yo oigo <u>con</u> mis <u>orejas</u>.

I eat ____ my _____.
Yo como <u>con</u> mi <u>boca</u>.

I taste ____ my _____.
Yo pruebo <u>con</u> mi <u>lengua</u>.

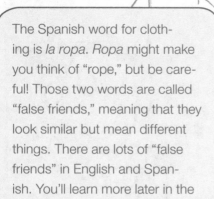

¿Cómo?—Say What?

The Spanish word for clothing is *la ropa*. *Ropa* might make you think of "rope," but be careful! Those two words are called "false friends," meaning that they look similar but mean different things. There are lots of "false friends" in English and Spanish. You'll learn more later in the book.

Clothes—*Ropa*

Wow, you've learned a lot of words to help you talk about the body so far. Now you just need to know how to talk about the clothes covering all those different parts of the body! Here are some words for clothes you probably have in your drawers and closet:

English	Spanish
a bathing suit	*un traje de baño*
a coat	*un abrigo*
a jacket	*una chaqueta*
some pajamas	*unas piyamas*
some pants	*unos pantalones*
a raincoat	*un impermeable*
some shorts	*unos shorts*
a sweater	*un suéter*
a T-shirt	*una camiseta*

Here are the Spanish words for some common boys' clothes:

English	Spanish
some boxer shorts	*unos calzoncillos*
a shirt	*una camisa*
a sports jacket	*una chaqueta sport*
a suit	*un traje*
a tie	*una corbata*
an undershirt	*una camiseta*
the underwear	*la ropa interior*

una camiseta

And here are the words for some girls' clothes:

English	Spanish
a bikini	*un biquini*
a blouse	*una blusa*
a bra	*un sostén*
a dress	*un vestido*
a nightgown	*un camisón*
some panties	*unas panties*
a skirt	*una falda*
some tights	*unas pantimedias*

Of course, most people wear other things besides just clothing. You might also wear jewelry or other accessories. Perhaps you wear a belt or a pair of glasses. Here are the Spanish words for all these things:

English	Spanish
a backpack	*una mochila*
a belt	*un cinturón*
a bracelet	*un brazalete*
some earrings	*unos aretes*
some glasses	*unas gafas*
some gloves	*unos guantes*
a hat	*un sombrero*
some mittens	*unos mitones*
a necklace	*un collar*
a purse	*una cartera*
a ring	*un anillo*
a scarf	*una bufanda*
some sunglasses	*unas gafas de sol*
a watch	*un reloj*
a wallet	*una billetera*

Here are some things you might wear on your feet:

English	Spanish
some boots	*unas botas*
some high-heeled shoes	*unos zapatos de tacones altos*
some sandals	*unas sandalias*
some shoes	*unos zapatos*
some slippers	*unas pantuflas*
some sneakers	*unos tenis*
some socks	*unos calcetines*

In English, you would use the word "wear" to tell someone what you're wearing, weather it's a shirt or a pair of shoes. But this is different in Spanish! The Spanish verb "to wear" is *llevar* for clothing and *calzar* for shoes. So, here's an example:

English	Spanish
I'm wearing shorts and a T-shirt and sandals.	*Llevo unos pantalones cortos y una camiseta y calzo unas sandalias.*

Now try describing the outfit you have on today. Fill in the blanks to create a complete sentence:

Llevo _____ *y* _____ *y calzo* _____.

To describe what someone else is wearing use the word *lleva*, which means "He (or She) is wearing." For example, if your mother is wearing a dress and a necklace, you would say *Lleva un vestido y un collar*. Keep creating new sentences using all the new words you learned in this chapter. Remember: The more you practice, the easier it will be!

CHAPTER 4
Places and Things—
Lugares y cosas

All Around Town

Find your way through the maze to learn the Spanish words for these familiar places! Start at the picture described in question number one. Find your way to the rest of the pictures. Write both the English and Spanish words on the lines provided.

1. Where do you borrow books?
2. Where do you study?
3. Where do you play?
4. Where do you mail a letter?
5. Where do you shop for food?

1._____

2._____

3._____

4._____

5._____

Shopping and Errands—*Compras y mandados*

There are all kinds of different stores and other places you might need to go to get your shopping and other errands done. Shopping for food can require a lot of different stops. Here are some places you might go to get the groceries you need:

English	Spanish
the bakery	*la panadería*
the butcher shop	*la carnicería*
the candy store	*la confitería*
the fruit stand	*la frutería*
the grocery store	*la tienda de comestibles*
the market	*el mercado*
the supermarket	*el supermercado*

Here are some sentences you might use when talking about shopping for food:

English	Spanish
I'm going to the bakery.	*Voy a la panadería.*
Let's go to the candy store.	*Vamos a la confitería.*

There are also lots of other places you might need to visit. Here are some examples:

English	Spanish
the bank	*el banco*
the barber	*la barbería*
the beauty shop	*la peluquería*
the church	*la iglesia*
the clothing store	*la tienda de ropa*
the department store	*la tienda por departamentos*

¡CUIDADO!
Mistake to Avoid

What's the difference between a grocery store, a market, and a supermarket? Well, a supermarket is a huge store that sells all kinds of fresh, boxed, and canned food, plus has special sections like a deli counter and bakery. A grocery store is a small, local store that sells food and things, and a market usually sells food outside, like a stand at a farmer's market.

Diversión—Fun Stuff

Do you know where the post office is in your town? The library? The school? Draw a map of your town and label in Spanish all the different buildings. If your town doesn't have all of the places on the list, you can make some up!

English	Spanish
the dentist	*el dentista*
the doctor	*el médico*
the dry cleaner	*la tintorería*
the eye doctor	*el oftalmólogo*
the hardware store	*la ferretería*
the laundromat	*la lavandería*
the library	*la biblioteca*
the pharmacy	*la farmacia*
the post office	*la oficina de correos*
the bookstore	*la librería*

Transportation—*Transporte*

Now that you know where you're going, you just need to figure out how to get there! This is where transporation comes in. Transportation includes all the vehicles that take you places, like cars, buses, and bicycles.

With all of these different methods of transportation, you're going to use a new verb: *ir* (to go). The conjugations you might need for this verb are *yo voy* (I go), *tú vas* (you go), and *nosotros vamos* (we go). After the verb, you're going to use *en*, which means "in" or "by." For example:

English	Spanish
I'm going by car.	*Yo voy en automóvil.*
Are you going by train?	*¿Vas en tren?*
We're going in a plane.	*Nosotros vamos en avión.*

For walking, though, you don't use *en*. You use *a* instead:

English	Spanish
I'm walking.	*Voy a pie.*

Here are some common modes of transportation you might use to get where you need to go:

English	Spanish
the bicycle	*la bicicleta*
the boat	*el barco*
the bus	*el autobús*
the car	*el automóvil*
the ferry	*el transbordador*
the helicopter	*el helicóptero*
the jet ski	*la moto acuática*
the motorbike	*la moto*
the motorboat	*la lancha a motor*
the motorcycle	*la motocicleta*
the plane	*el avión*
the RV	*la caravana*
the sailboat	*el barco de vela*
the scooter	*el scooter, el ciclomotor*
the skateboard	*el monopatín*
the skates	*los patines*
the subway	*el metro*
the taxi	*el taxi*
the train	*el tren*
the tricycle	*el triciclo*
the truck	*el camión*
the van	*la camioneta*
walking	*a pie*

¿Cómo?— Say What?

In a discussion about transportation, you might also need to use some other words. Perhaps you have to buy a bus or train ticket before you can board. Here are some words that will help you: station—*la estación*; ticket—*el boleto*; to buy—*comprar*; to pay—*pagar*.

el autobús

Vacation—*Vacaciones*

Where do you like to go on vacation? The beach? The mountains? Around the world? Here is some Spanish vocabulary to help you find your way there—and back home.

Consejo
IMPORTANT TIP

If you're going to another country, there are a few extra words you'll need to know: customs—*la aduana;* immigration—*la inmigración;* passport—*el pasaporte;* visa—*un visado/una visa.*

English	Spanish
Where are you going?	¿Adónde vas?
I'm going . . .	Voy . . .
to an amusement park	a un parque de atracciones
to my grandparents' house	a la casa de mis abuelos
to the beach	a la playa
to the city	a la ciudad
to the mountains	a las montañas
to the rainforest	al bosque tropical
overseas	al extranjero

Here are a couple of examples:

English	Spanish
I'm going to the beach.	Voy a la playa.
I'm going overseas.	Voy al extranjero.

When you travel long distances, you sometimes have to fly in an airplane. Here's some vocabulary to use at the airport:

English	Spanish
the airport	el aeropuerto
Arrivals	Llegadas
the baggage	el equipaje
the baggage claim	el reclamo de equipaje
the boarding pass	la tarjeta de embarque
the carry-on luggage	el equipaje de mano
the duty-free store	la tienda libre de impuestos
the check-in desk	el mostrador de registro
Departures	Salidas
the economy (coach) class	la clase económica
the first class	la primera clase
the flight	un vuelo
a gate	una puerta de embarque

English	Spanish
a layover	*una escala*
a one-way ticket	*un boleto de ida*
a plane ticket	*un boleto de avión*
a round-trip ticket	*un boleto de ida y vuelta*
a security check	*el control de seguridad*
a shuttle	*un servicio de autobús*
a terminal	*la terminal*

Here are some verbs to use at the airport:

English	Spanish
to board	*embarcar*
to buy a ticket	*comprar un boleto*
to land	*aterrizar*
to make a reservation	*hacer una reservación*
to take off	*despegar*

Once you've arrived at your destination, you can help your parents or other family members by knowing the following helpful words and phrases:

English	Spanish
Where is . . . ?	*¿Dónde está . . . ?*
the bank	*el banco*
the bathroom	*el baño*
the church	*la iglesia*
the currency exchange	*el cambio de moneda*
the hospital	*el hospital*
the hotel	*el hotel*
the movie theater	*el cine*
the museum	*el museo*
the park	*el parque*
the police station	*la comisaría*

Gotta Go!

You have just traveled a long way, and you need to go—quick! Use the directions to cross out words in the grid. Read the leftover words from top to bottom and left to right. That's the polite way to ask directions to the bathroom!

Cross out: *números* • *familia* • *colores*

Can you add the correct punctuation? Remember to think upside-down!

UNO	DÓNDE	EL HIJO
ESTÁ	PAPÁ	OCHO
ROJO	EL	AZUL
LA TÍA	SEIS	BAÑO
POR	VERDE	FAVOR

la escuela

English	Spanish
the pool	*la piscina*
the post office	*la oficina de correos*
the restaurant	*el restaurante*
the school	*la escuela*
the theater	*el teatro*

Now pretend that you're at your vacation destination and you need to ask where some different places are. Remember the words and phrases you just learned and complete some sentences asking where different places are. For example, if you want to know where the post office is, you would ask *¿Dónde está la oficina de correos?* Try it out:

¿Dónde está? _____

¿Dónde está? _____

¿Dónde está? _____

¿Dónde está? _____

¿Dónde está? _____

When you and your family are trying to get somewhere, you'll also need to talk about directions and locations. For instance, you might need to go through the door on the left, visit the counter in front of the escalator, or travel west on the highway. Here are some words that will help you talk about direction and location:

¡CUIDADO!
Mistake to Avoid

The Spanish words for "east" and "west" are kind of similar, so be sure to pronounce them correctly. *Este* (east) is pronounced ES teh, and *oeste* (west) is pronounced oh ES teh—don't forget to say that *o* at the beginning, which is pronounced like "oh"!

English	Spanish
It is . . .	*Está . . .*
To the left	*a la izquierda*
To the right	*a la derecha*
straight ahead	*hacia adelante*

English	Spanish
next to	*junto a*
in front of	*enfrente de*
in back of	*detrás de*
up	*arriba*
down	*abajo*
near	*cerca*
far	*lejos*
north	*norte*
south	*sur*
east	*este*
west	*oeste*

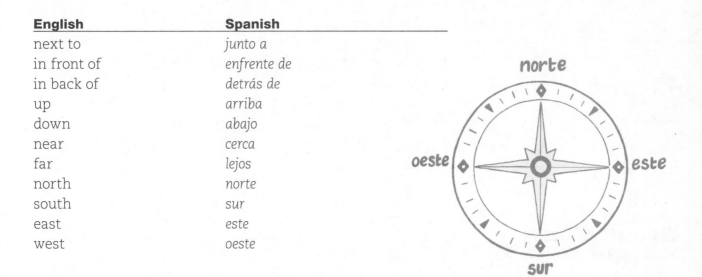

Colors—*Colores*

Now it's time to talk about colors! Knowing how to say all the colors in Spanish will help you describe the things you see. Perhaps there is a blue mailbox down the street or a red bird in the tree. Once you know all these words, you can describe almost anything!

English	Spanish
red	*rojo*
purple	*violeta*
blue	*azul*
green	*verde*
yellow	*amarillo*
orange	*naranja*
black	*negro*
white	*blanco*
gray	*gris*
brown	*marrón/café*
pink	*rosado*

Diversión_Fun Stuff

Write the Spanish words for all the colors on small stickers and use them to label your crayons, pens, markers, and paints. This will help you remember these new words!

One important difference in Spanish is that adjectives like colors come after the noun, instead of before it, like in English. In the following examples, notice how the color comes before the noun in English but after it in Spanish:

English	Spanish
My mom has a blue car.	*Mi mamá tiene un automóvil azul.*
I have a red bike.	*Tengo una bicicleta roja.*

Do you see how the word *roja* was used to describe *bicicleta*? This is because *bicicleta* is a feminine word (it ends in *a*). Remember to change the ending to *a* if the word you're describing is feminine. The colors *violeta* and *naranja* are always used with the ending *a*.

Now use the Spanish words for colors to describe some of the different things you have. These are all words you've already learned, so you just have to remember what they mean and then add a color in the blank space. Remember to change the ending on the color word to match the gender of the word your describing, if necessary.

una bicicleta _____

una mochila _____

un suéter _____

una camiseta _____

Now that you know how to talk about colors in Spanish, go tell your family what your favorite color is. Start with *Mi color favorito es* and then add the color. So, if your favorite color is red, just say *Mi color favorito es el rojo.* It's easy!

Gramática —
Additional Grammar

To describe a color as "light" or "dark," you need to know the words *claro* (light) and *oscuro* (dark). For example: light gray—*gris claro;* light green—*verde claro;* dark red—*rojo oscuro;* dark brown—*café oscuro.*

Shapes—*Formas*

Now you know how to describe things by their color, but what about their shape? Circles, ovals, and triangles are common shapes. Here are some shape words to help you describe what you see around you:

English	Spanish
an arch	*un arco*
a circle	*un círculo*
a cone	*un cono*
a crescent	*una media luna*
a cube	*un cubo*
a curve	*una curva*
a cylinder	*un cilindro*
a diamond	*un diamante*
a heart	*un corazón*
a hexagon	*un hexágono*
a line	*una línea*
an octagon	*un octágono*
an oval	*un óvalo*
a pentagon	*un pentágono*
a pyramid	*una pirámide*
a rectangle	*un rectángulo*
a sphere	*una esfera*
a square	*un cuadrado*
a star	*una estrella*
a triangle	*un triángulo*

Sizes—*Tamaños*

While color and shape are good ways to describe things, you can also talk about size. Here are some good size words to know:

¿Cómo?— Say What?

Did you know that there are different categories of shapes? Shapes like *círculos* and *cuadrados* are two-dimensional, bi-dimensional, which means they're flat. Shapes like *esferas* and *cubos* are three-dimensional (3-D), *tridimensional*, so you can actually hold them in your hand and see all their sides.

Diversión—Fun Stuff

Don't forget the best shape of all! The Spanish word for "rainbow" is *arco iris*. Draw a rainbow and label each stripe with the Spanish word for that color. ROY G. BIV is a trick to help you remember the colors: red, orange, yellow, green, blue, indigo (dark blue), and violet.

Gramática —
Additional Grammar

To say that something is more ____, or that it's ____-er than something else, you use the word *más* (more) in Spanish. For example, to say "The dog is bigger than the cat," say *El perro es más grande que el gato.* To say, "I want a smaller book," say, *Quiero un libro más pequeño.*

Consejo
IMPORTANT TIP

There are other quantity words that are less specific but just as useful: *mucho* (a lot), *muchísimo* (a whole lot), *un poquito* (a little), *más* (more), and *menos* (less).

English	Spanish
huge	*enorme*
large/big	*grande*
long	*largo*
medium	*mediano*
narrow	*estrecho*
short	*corto*
small	*pequeño*
tiny	*pequeñito*
wide	*ancho*

In Spanish, not only are there different words for weights and distances, but there is also a different system of measurement. Americans use the "English system," which includes inches, feet, miles, pounds, gallons, and so on. Most of the rest of the world uses the "metric system."

To measure distance, the metric system uses "meters." One meter (*un metro*) is a little more than three feet. One kilometer (*un kilómetro*) is just over half a mile. A centimeter (*un centímetro*) is one hundredth of a meter; 2½ centimeters equal one inch.

For weight, the metric system uses "grams." Thirty-two grams (*gramos*) equal about an ounce (*una onza*). A kilogram (*un kilogramo*) equals 2.2 pounds.

The metric system measures volume with "liters." One liter (*un litro*) is a bit more than a quart.

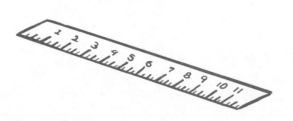

CHAPTER 5
At Home—*En la casa*

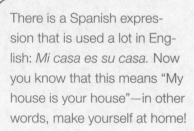

¿Cómo?— Say What?

There is a Spanish expression that is used a lot in English: *Mi casa es su casa*. Now you know that this means "My house is your house"—in other words, make yourself at home!

Diversión—Fun Stuff

Want a fun way to practice your house vocabulary? Draw a big picture of your house and label all of the rooms, spaces, and furniture with their Spanish names. Keep adding to your picture as you learn more words later in this chapter.

Rooms and Furniture—*Cuartos y muebles*

When you're at home—*en la casa*—you can use this Spanish vocabulary to explain where you are and what your house is like. Here are rooms and other places and things you might find in your home:

English	Spanish
the attic	*el ático*
the balcony	*el balcón*
the basement	*el sótano*
the bathroom	*el baño*
the bedroom	*el dormitorio*
the ceiling	*el techo*
the den	*el estudio*
the dining room	*el comedor*
the door	*la puerta*
the floor	*el piso*
the hall	*el pasillo*
the kitchen	*la cocina*
the porch	*la terraza*
the room	*el cuarto, la pieza*
the screen door	*la puerta mosquitera*
the stairway	*la escalera*
the study	*el despacho*
the wall	*la pared*
the window	*la ventana*

Once you know what all of the different rooms and spaces are called, you can fill them up with furniture and other things.

English	Spanish
a bookshelf	*una estantería*
a carpet	*una alfombra*
a chair	*una silla*
a computer	*una computadora*
a couch	*un sofá*
a curtain	*una cortina*
a desk	*un escritorio*
a dryer	*una secadora*
a lamp	*una lámpara*
a poster	*un cartel*
a printer	*una impresora*
a rug	*un tapete, una alfombra*
a stereo	*un estéreo*
a table	*una mesa*
a telephone	*un teléfono*
a television set	*un televisor*
a washer	*una lavadora*

el teléfono

Here are some things found in the bathroom:

English	Spanish
a bathtub	*una bañera, un baño*
a mirror	*un espejo*
a shower	*una ducha*
a sink	*un lavamanos*

Here's what you might find in the bedroom:

English	Spanish
an alarm clock	*un despertador*
a bed	*una cama*
a closet	*un clóset*
a dresser	*un tocador*

My Room

If your bedroom had a large, blank *pared* (wall), what could you use to decorate it? Use the decoder to find out! Extra fun: Use brightly colored markers to write the answer letters on top of the coded letters. Then turn the letters into the kind of wall decoration this puzzle is about!

UN
CARTEL

A = O
C = P
E = E
L = R
UN = A
R = S
T = T

el fútbol

What else does this boy have in his room? Collect the letters in order from *uno* to *siete* and find out!

Outside—*Afuera*

You might have lots of different things outside your house too, like a yard, sidewalk, or driveway. Use this vocabulary to explain what the outside of your house is like in Spanish.

English	Spanish
the woods	el bosque
the doghouse	la caseta del perro
the driveway	la entrada del automóvil
the fence	la valla
the flower	la flor
the garage	el garaje
the garden	el jardín
the gate	el portón
the hammock	la hamaca
the hose	la manguera
the mailbox	el buzón
the parking space	el estacionamiento
the path	el camino
the patio	el patio
the road	la calle
the sandbox	el cajón de arena
the sidewalk	la acera
the slide	el tobogán
the swing	el columpio
the trail	el sendero
the tree	el árbol
the yard	el jardín

¡CUIDADO!
Mistake to Avoid

Be careful with the Spanish word *tobogán*. It can mean a slide, like in a playground or into a swimming pool, and it can also mean a toboggan or sled for the snow.

el árbol

Go outside and see which of these items are in your yard. Look all around the yard and write down the Spanish words for the different things you find in the following blank spaces:

_____

_____

_____

_____

_____

Everyday Actions—*Todos los días*

There are some things that you do every day, or almost every day, so you need to be able to talk about that stuff, too.

English	Spanish
to wake up	*despertarse*
to get up	*levantarse*
to get tired	*cansarse*
to go to bed	*acostarse*
to fall asleep	*dormirse*
to get ready	*arreglarse*
to take a bath	*bañarse*
to take a shower	*ducharse*
to wash (up)	*lavarse*
to get dressed	*vestirse*
to put on clothes	*ponerse*
to brush (hair, teeth)	*cepillarse*
to comb (hair)	*peinarse*
to take off clothes	*quitarse*

Consejo
IMPORTANT TIP

Here are a couple of extra verbs to describe what your parents might do every day: to put on makeup—*maquillarse, pintarse;* to shave—*afeitarse.*

A verb with *se* at the end needs an extra word when you conjugate it. So for *cansarse*, you would say *Yo me canso* (I'm getting tired) and *¿Tú te cansas?* (Are you getting tired)?

Here are some sample sentences using these kinds of verbs:

English	Spanish
I'm washing up.	*Me lavo.*
I'm taking a bath.	*Me baño.*
I'm brushing my teeth.	*Me cepillo los dientes.*

Chores—*Quehaceres domésticos*

Don't forget to do your chores! Here are some chore verbs that will come in handy as you and your family are taking care of things around the house:

English	Spanish
to cook	*cocinar*
to do laundry	*lavar la ropa*
to do the dishes	*lavar los platos*
to do the shopping	*hacer las compras*
to make the bed	*hacer la cama*
to mop the floor	*fregar el piso*
to mow the lawn	*cortar el césped*
to put the house in order	*arreglar la casa*
to straighten up	*poner en orden*
to sweep the floor	*barrer el piso*
to take out the garbage	*sacar la basura*
to vacuum	*pasar la aspiradora*

Gramática —
Additional Grammar

To say that you have to do a certain chore, use *Tengo que* plus that expression. For example, if you have to do the dishes, you would say *Tengo que lavar los platos.*

Chores aren't always very fun, are they? Well, here's a way to make chores more interesting: Make a list of the chores that you have to do, but in Spanish! Fill in the following blanks to create a complete chore list. Your parents will be so impressed with your Spanish and your hard work!

1. _____

2. _____

3. _____

4. _____

5. _____

Pets—*Animales domésticos*

A good pet can be like a member of the family, so be sure you know the word for your pet in Spanish. Here are some types of pets and their Spanish translations:

English	Spanish
an ant	*una hormiga*
a bird	*un pájaro*
a cat	*un gato*
a dog	*un perro*
a ferret	*un hurón*
a fish	*un pez*
a frog	*una rana*
a gerbil	*un gerbo*
a guinea pig	*un cobayo*
a hamster	*un hámster*
a hermit crab	*un cangrejo ermitaño*
a horse	*un caballo*

el gato

¡CUIDADO!
Mistake to Avoid

Rata and *ratón* both look like they could mean "rat," so you need to make a special effort to remember that *ratón* means mouse, as in *el Ratón Mickey* (Mickey Mouse). *Rata* is actually the word for rat in Spanish.

English	Spanish
a mouse	*un ratón*
a rabbit	*un conejo*
a rat	*una rata*
a snake	*una serpiente*
a tarantula	*una tarántula*
a turtle	*una tortuga*

Do you already have a pet? If so, what kind? Write a complete sentence saying what kind of pet you have. You'll start with the word *Tengo*, which means I have. For example, "I have a turtle" is *Tengo una tortuga* in Spanish.

Tengo _____ .

If you don't already have a pet, do you want one? To say that you want something, you start with *Quiero*. So, to say "I want a dog," you would say, *Quiero un perro*. Use the following to complete such a sentence:

Quiero _____ .

This, That, These, Those—*Este/Esta, Ese/Esa, Estos/Estas, Esos/Esas*

The words this, that, these, and those are used to demonstrate things or people. In English, as well as in Spanish you use them before the things or people you are referring to. They change a little depending on whether the next word is singular, plural, feminine, or masculine.

> **Diversión—Fun Stuff**
>
> If you could have any pet you wanted, what would it be? *¿Un pájaro? ¿Un caballo?* And where would it live? *¿Afuera? ¿En la cocina? ¿En tu cama?*

▼   **MASCULINE SINGULAR AND PLURAL**

English	Spanish	Pronunciation
This	Este	EHS teh
That	Ese	EHS eh
These	Estos	EHS tohs
Those	Esos	EHS ohs

▼   **FEMININE SINGULAR AND PLURAL**

English	Spanish	Pronunciation
This	Esta	EHS tah
That	Esa	EHS ah
These	Estas	EHS tahs
Those	Esas	EHS ahs

Here are some examples using these words:

English	Spanish
That girl is pretty.	Esa muchacha es bonita.
Those boys are tall.	Esos muchachos son altos.
These telephones are black.	Estos teléfonos son negros.

Now you try with the following sentences:

English	Spanish
Those frogs are green.	_____ ranas son verdes.
This cat is mine.	_____ gato es mío.
That turtle is slow.	_____ tortuga es lenta.

CHAPTER 6

School and Work—
Escuela y trabajo

¿Cómo?— Say What?

Even though the word *mapa* ends in *a*, it's masculine, not feminine. There are a few other words like this as well, including *un día* (a day), *un problema* (a problem), and *un programa* (a program). You have to make an extra effort to remember these words that don't follow the rule!

Diversión—Fun Stuff

Chances are, one of your favorite times of the day is probably recess, which is called *el recreo* in Spanish, and a playground is *un patio de recreo*. Some things you might find in a playground are *un columpio* (swing), *un tobogán* (slide), *un cajón de arena* (sandbox), and *una trepadora* (jungle gym).

At School—*En la escuela*

Right now, your job is to go to school. You probably learn about all different subjects at school and use lots of different tools to do your work. Here are some Spanish words to help you talk about your job as a student.

English	Spanish
a school	*una escuela*
a high school	*una escuela secundaria*
a college	*una universidad*
a backpack	*una mochila*
a calculator	*una calculadora*
chalk	*una tiza*
a chalkboard	*una pizarra*
a class	*una clase*
a classroom	*un aula*
the crayons	*los lápices de color*
a desk	*un pupitre*
the glue	*la goma*
a homework	*una tarea*
a map	*un mapa*
a notebook	*un cuaderno*
a ruler	*una regla*
the scissors	*las tijeras*
a tape	*una cinta adhesiva*
a test	*un examen*
a quiz	*una prueba corta / un quiz*

las tijeras

Classes—*Clases*

Your job as a student can include all kinds of interesting classes. Here are some of the subjects you might be studying.

English	Spanish
art	*arte*
biology	*biología*
chemistry	*química*
civics	*educación cívica*
English	*inglés*
French	*francés*
geography	*geografía*
German	*alemán*
gym, physical education	*educación física*
history	*historia*
home economics	*economía doméstica*
Latin	*latín*
math	*matemáticas*
music	*música*
science	*ciencia*
social studies	*estudios sociales*
Spanish	*español*

You probably like some classes in school more than others, right? What is your favorite class? To answer this question in Spanish, you would say *Mi clase favorita es* . . . Give it a try:

Mi clase favorita es _____.

Gramática — Additional Grammar

There are two Spanish words that mean language, one is masculine and the other one is feminine: *el idioma* and *la lengua.* If you use *el idioma* you need to say the name of the language in the masculine form and if you use *la lengua* then the name of the language would be in the feminine form: *el idioma español, la lengua española;—el idioma inglés, la lengua inglesa;—el idioma francés, la lengua francesa;* and so on.

¿Cómo?— Say What?

There are two different words for "letter" in Spanish, because there are two different kinds of letters. A letter of the alphabet is called *una letra*, while a letter that you write to a friend is called *una carta*.

Reading and Writing—*Lectura y escritura*

Reading and writing are two things that you have to do in almost all of your classes. Here are some of the things you'll need.

English	Spanish
a book	*un libro*
a dictionary	*un diccionario*
an eraser	*un borrador*
a paper	*el papel*
a pen	*una pluma*
a pencil	*un lápiz*
the reading	*la lectura*
to read	*leer*
a spelling	*la ortografía*
How do you spell _____?	*¿Cómo se escribe _____?*
the writing	*la escritura*
to write	*escribir*
to write in cursive	*escribir en cursiva*
an accent	*un acento*

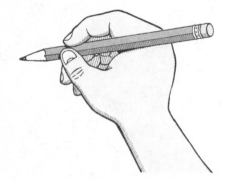

Consejo
IMPORTANT TIP

Papel refers to paper in general, like if you want to say "I don't have any paper" (*No tengo papel*). When you want to talk about a piece of paper, you would say *una hoja de papel* or *un trozo de papel*. For example, "I need a piece of paper" would be *Necesito una hoja de papel*. Another interesting fact is that the word *hoja* means leaf, so when you say *una hoja de papel*, you're literally saying a leaf of paper. This is what the term "loose-leaf" paper refers to!

Reading List

Use the clues to fill a letter into each empty box. When you are done, you'll have a Spanish word that answers this silly riddle:

What do all students need to read?

☐	letter right after T
☐	letter just before O
☐	letter between K and M
☐	the ninth letter
☐	the second letter
☐	the second letter after P
☐	letter right after N

On the Computer—*En la computadora*

You probably do a lot of work (and play) on the computer. Here is the Spanish vocabulary you need to talk about the computer:

English	Spanish
a CD-ROM	*un CD-ROM*
a computer	*una computadora*
a database	*una base de datos*
a disk drive	*una unidad de disco*
a file	*un archivo*
a hard drive	*un disco duro*
a hardware	*un hardware*
a keyboard	*un teclado*
a laptop (computer)	*una computadora portátil*
a monitor	*un monitor*
a mouse	*un ratón*
a to print	*imprimir*

English	Spanish
a printer	*una impresora*
to save	*archivar*
the software	*el software*
a spell checker	*el corrector ortográfico*
to type	*escribir a máquina*
a word processor	*un procesador de textos*
a videogame	*un videojuego*

And of course what would a computer be without the Internet and e-mail?

English	Spanish
the e-mail	*el correo electrónico*
the e-mail address	*la dirección electrónica*
the Internet	*el Internet*
an Internet browser	*un navegador*
an Internet café	*un café Internet*
a search engine	*un motor de búsqueda*
a web page	*una página web*
a website	*un sitio web*

Jobs—*Trabajos*

Right now your job is to go to school, but when you grow up, you'll have a different job. Perhaps you've thought about becoming a firefighter or a pilot. Here are the Spanish words for some cool careers:

English	Spanish
an actor/actress	*un actor/una actriz*
an artist	*un/una artista*
a baker	*un panadero/una panadera*

¡CUIDADO!
Mistake to Avoid

Even though CD-ROM looks the same in Spanish and English, it's pronounced differently: "see dee rom" in English, but "se de rom" in Spanish.

Diversión_Fun Stuff

If you don't have an e-mail address and would like to create one, or if you have one and would like to change it, why not try making one in Spanish? For example, if you like cats, you might create an address like gatos123@yahoo.com. If you like the color blue, you might choose azul_is_cool@hotmail.com. Ask your parent for help when you do this.

English	Spanish
a butcher	*un carnicero, una carnicera*
a carpenter	*un carpintero, una carpintera*
a cashier	*un cajero, una cajera*
a cook	*un cocinero, una cocinera*
a doctor	*un doctor, una doctora*
an electrician	*un/una electricista*
an employee	*un empleado, una empleada*
an engineer	*un ingeniero, una ingeniera*
a fireman	*un bombero, una bombera*
a flight attendant	*un/una auxiliar de vuelo*
a lawyer	*un abogado, una abogada*
a maid	*una empleada doméstica*
a mail carrier	*un cartero, una cartera*
a manager	*un/una gerente*
a mechanic	*un mecánico, una mecánica*
a nurse	*un enfermero, una enfermera*
a pilot	*un/una piloto*
a plumber	*un plomero, una plomera*
a police officer	*un/una policía*
a receptionist	*un/una recepcionista*
secretary	*un secretario, una secretaria*
student	*un/una estudiante*
teacher	*un profesor, una profesora*
waiter/waitress	*un camarero, una camarera*
writer	*un escritor, una escritora*

Consejo
IMPORTANT TIP

When talking about most jobs, you have to explain whether the person is a man or a woman. Sometimes the word itself is the same; for example, *piloto* is the same for men and women. But the article always shows the difference: *un piloto* (man) and *una piloto* (woman).

Dressed for Work

What is *el bombero* (the fireman) wearing to work? Going from left to right, cross out the letters that spell the English word for each thing. Color the leftover letters to learn the Spanish word!

EL **HCEALSMCEOT**

EL **ACBROIGAOT**

LOS **GGULAONVTESES**

LOS **PPAANNTTALONESS**

LAS **BBOOOTTASS**

EXTRA FUN: Who is the fireman's friend?

EL **DPEORRGO**

At the Office—*En la oficina*

Many people work in offices, so this last section on jobs includes lots of vocabulary to help you find your way around the office.

¿Cómo?— Say What?

Remember *un pupitre* from the section on school? That's a special kind of desk found in classrooms. But a regular desk, like adults use, is called *un escritorio.*

English	Spanish
a briefcase	*un maletín*
a calculator	*una calculadora*
a chair	*una silla*
a copy machine	*una copiadora*
a desk	*un escritorio*
a fax machine	*un máquina de fax*
a file folder	*una carpeta*
a filing cabinet	*un archivador*
a highlighter	*un marcador*
a index card	*una ficha*
the mail	*el correo*
a office	*una oficina*
a paper clip	*un clip*
a rubber band	*una banda elástica*
a staple	*una grapa*
a stapler	*una grapadora*
a telephone	*un teléfono*
a typewriter	*una máquina de escribir*

¡CUIDADO! Mistake to Avoid

Be careful with *carpeta* and *grapa*—they don't mean "carpet" and "grape," but rather "folder" and "staple." These are just two of many "false friends" in English and Spanish.

Did you know that some people do their work from home? Maybe you have a parent who does this from an office right in your house. Whether your parents work at home or someplace else, chances are you have some office supplies in different places in your house. Let's take a look around!

The following list contains the Spanish words for different office supplies. If you can't remember what a word means, look back at the vocabulary lists that appear earlier in this chapter. Search around your house until you find each of the items in the list. Then, fill in the blank spaces with the room or rooms where you found each item and how many you found. Here's the tricky part: You must write down the rooms and the numbers in Spanish! Go back to Chapter 5 if you're having trouble remembering how to say the different rooms in Spanish. The first one is done as an example.

Item in Spanish	Location(s)	Number of Items Found
un teléfono	la cocina	uno
una goma		
una grapa		
un clip		
un ratón		
una grapadora		
una pluma		
una ficha		
un marcador		
unas tijeras		
una calculadora		
una computadora		

CHAPTER 7
Time and Dates—
Hora y fechas

Son las tres y media

What Time Is It?—*¿Qué hora es?*

Telling time in Spanish is very easy, as long as you know your numbers. Good thing you're a numbers expert since reading Chapter 1, right? If you need to refresh your memory, go back and revisit that part of the book for a few minutes.

To ask what time it is, just say *¿Qué hora es?* Then to answer, you say *son las* and then the number. Here are some examples:

English	Spanish
It's two o'clock.	*Son las dos.*
It's three o'clock.	*Son las tres.*

To say that it's something "thirty," use *media* (half).

English	Spanish
It's 3:30.	*Son las tres y media.*
It's 4:30.	*Son las cuatro y media.*

When you're talking about time, the word "quarter" means a span of fifteen minutes. To say that it's quarter after or quarter to in Spanish, use y *cuarto* (quarter after) or *menos cuarto* (quarter to).

English	Spanish
It's 5:15.	*Son las cinco y cuarto.*
It's 6:15.	*Son las seis y cuarto.*
It's 6:45.	*Son las siete menos cuarto.*
It's 7:45.	*Son las ocho menos cuarto.*

For other times, like ten after and five to, you'll use either y (if it's time added on to the hour) or *menos* (if it's time substracted from the hour), plus the the number.

English	Spanish
It's 8:10.	*Son las ocho y diez.*
It's 9:20.	*Son las nueve y veinte.*
It's 10:55.	*Son las once menos cinco.*
It's 11:40.	*Son las doce menos veinte.*

Talking about A.M. and P.M. is a little different in Spanish. For A.M., you can use *de la mañana* (in the morning): *Son las seis de la mañana* (It's six A.M.) But for P.M., you have two choices: *de la tarde* (in the afternoon), when talking about anywhere from noon to about 6 P.M., and *de la noche* (in the evening or at night), for 6 P.M. to midnight. Here are some examples:

English	Spanish
It's 1 p.m. It's 1 in the afternoon.	*Es la una de la tarde.*
It's 7 p.m. It's 7 in the evening.	*Son las seis de la noche.*
It's 11 p.m. It's 11 at night.	*Son las once de la noche.*

Days, Months, and Seasons—*Días, meses, y estaciones*

The Spanish days of the week are very different from the English ones:

English	Spanish
Monday	*lunes*
Tuesday	*martes*
Wednesday	*miércoles*
Thursday	*jueves*
Friday	*viernes*
Saturday	*sábado*
Sunday	*domingo*

Consejo
IMPORTANT TIP

There are three occasions where you use *es* instead of *son* when you're talking about time: It's one o'clock—*Es la una.* It's noon—*Es mediodía.* It's midnight—*Es medianoche.* Also, if you want to say that something will be happening at a certain time, you use the word *a*, which means "at" in Spanish. For example, "at seven o'clock" is *a las siete.*

¿Cómo?—Say What?

The Spanish week starts on Monday instead of Sunday. In addition, days of the week are not capitalized in Spanish the way they are in English.

Now that you know how to tell time and say the days of the week in Spanish, it's time to practice what you've learned. Make a schedule of your typical day, with the times and everything you do written in Spanish. For example, you might list waking up in the morning, eating breakfast, and taking a shower before school. Revisit the section called Everyday Actions—*Todos los días* in Chapter 5 if you need help remembering how to say certain daily activities. Here's a sample of what one entry in your schedule might look like:

El día (day)	*La hora* (time)	*La actividad* (activity)
lunes	a las siete de la mañana	despertarse

Here are the words for the months of the year—*los meses del año*:

English	Spanish
January	*enero*
February	*febrero*
March	*marzo*
April	*abril*
May	*mayo*
June	*junio*
July	*julio*
August	*agosto*
September	*septiembre*
October	*octubre*
November	*noviembre*
December	*diciembre*

¡CUIDADO!
Mistake to Avoid

Like days of the week, months are not capitalized in Spanish. Of course, if the day of the week or the month comes at the beginning of the sentence, it would be capitalized: *Fui a Mexico en mayo* (I went to Mexico in May). *Agosto tiene treinta y un días* (There are thirty-one days in August).

Here are the words for the four seasons in Spanish:

English	Spanish
the spring	*la primavera*
the summer	*el verano*
the autumn	*el otoño*
the winter	*el invierno*

What's your favorite season of the year?
Why? A little later in this chapter, you'll learn
how to talk about weather. This will help you
describe your favorite season to your friends!

What's Today's Date?—*¿Cuál es la fecha de hoy?*

Talking about the date in Spanish is a little bit tricky. To ask
"What's the date?" say *¿Cuál es la fecha?* Then you can answer
with *Es el* (It is) plus the date.

Here are some examples:

English	Spanish
It's October 2.	*Es el 2 de octubre.*
It's March 15.	*Es el 15 de marzo.*
It's December 31.	*Es el 31 de diciembre.*

On the first day of the month, instead of saying *uno*, in
Spanish you say *primero*, just like how in English you'd say
January 1st, not January 1.

English	Spanish
It's May 1st.	*Es el primero de mayo.*
It's July 1st.	*Es el primero de julio.*

Gramática —
Additional Grammar

Here are three things that are different about dates in Spanish: (1) The definite article (*el*) is used in front of the date; (2) The number always goes in front of the month; (3) *De* goes between the date and month.

When you write the short form of the date in Spanish, the day still goes before the month:

English	Spanish
May 30 (5/30)	*mayo 30 (30/5)*
January 20 (1/20)	*enero 20 (20/1)*

Some dates can be really tricky:

English	Spanish
February 3 (2/3)	*febrero 3 (3/2)*
March 2 (3/2)	*marzo 2 (2/3)*

So, you really need to remember that the day goes first in Spanish, otherwise you might get the date completely wrong!

Weather—*Tiempo*

To talk about the weather, you need to learn a new verb: *hacer*. When followed by weather words related to temperature and the sky, *hacer* means "to be." And the only conjugation you need is *hace* (it is). Here are some important sentences to know:

English	Spanish
How's the weather?	*¿Qué tiempo hace?*
It's bad weather.	*Hace mal tiempo.*
It's cold.	*Hace frío.*
It's cool.	*Está fresco.*
It's hot.	*Hace calor.*
It's nice out.	*Hace buen tiempo.*

As always, there are exceptions. There are times when the verb *hace* doesn't work. In those cases you need to use different verbs. Here are some examples:

It's cloudy.	*Está nublado.*
It's cool.	*Está fresco.*
It's sunny.	*Hay sol o está soleado.*
It's foggy.	*Hay neblina.*

To talk about specific temperatures, you'll also use *hace*:

English	Spanish
It's 70 degrees.	*Hace setenta grados.*
It's 5 degrees below zero.	*Hace cinco grados bajo cero.*

For rain, snow, and hail, you need to use *está* (it is):

English	Spanish
It's raining.	*Está lloviendo.*
It's snowing.	*Está nevando.*
It's hailing.	*Está cayendo granizo.*

And finally, when you want to say that there is a very severe weather condition like a blizzard, use *hay* (there is) plus the word:

English	Spanish
a blizzard	*una ventisca*
a drought	*una sequía*
a flood	*una inundación*
a hurricane	*un huracán*
a tornado	*un tornado*

Consejo
IMPORTANT TIP

For temperatures, most countries use Celsius, which can be confusing if you're not used to it. To convert from Fahrenheit to Celsius, take the Fahrenheit temperature, subtract 30, and divide by 2. This will give you an approximate Celsius temperature. For example, 70°F - 30 = 40 ÷ 2 = 20°C. To convert from Celsius to Fahrenheit, it's just the opposite: multiply by 2 and add 30: 10°C × 2 = 20 + 30 = 50°F.

Holidays—*Días festivos*

Everybody likes to celebrate, but holidays are not the same in every country. Here are some holidays that are celebrated in the United States as well as in many Spanish-speaking countries:

English	Spanish
Christmas	*la Navidad*
Christmas Eve	*la Nochebuena*
Easter	*la Pascua*
Father's Day	*el Día del Padre*
Mother's Day	*el Día de la Madre*
New Year's	*el Año Nuevo*
New Year's Eve	*el Fin de Año*
Valentine's Day	*el Día de San Valentín*

Birthdays—*Cumpleaños*

For many people, birthdays are the most special days of all! Here are some useful phrases for talking about your own birthday, as well as those of your friends and family.

English	Spanish
a birthday	*un cumpleaños*
a birthday cake	*una torta de cumpleaños*
a birthday card	*una tarjeta de cumpleaños*
a birthday party	*una fiesta de cumpleaños*
a birthday present	*un regalo de cumpleaños*
Happy birthday!	*¡Feliz cumpleaños!*

In Hispanic countries, a girl's fifteenthth birthday is the most special. The closest equivalent in the United States is the now old-fashioned coming-out party. In Mexico and other Hispanic countries, fifteen is seen as the age when a girl turns into a woman, and this is commemorated with a huge party, with many similarities to a wedding in the United States, with a church ceremony, a fancy white or light pink dress and matching bouquet, a "court" with *damas* (maids of honor) and *chambelanes* (gentlemen), party favors, and a

Diversión—Fun Stuff

Make a calendar using all of your new vocabulary, either with a pen and paper or on the computer. Make a page for each month and label the months and days of the week in Spanish, then add all of the holidays celebrated in Spanish-speaking countries as well as in your own. And don't forget birthdays!

Consejo
IMPORTANT TIP

In the United States, a girl's "sweet sixteenthth" birthday is considered the most special. But even the fanciest sweet-sixteen party is nowhere near as elaborate as *la quinceañera.*

banquet. This party is called *la Fiesta de quince años*. The girl turning fifteen is called *la quinceañera*.

To ask "How old are you?" say *¿Cuántos años tienes?*

And then to answer, you need to use *tengo*, from the verb *tener* (which normally means "to have") plus the number and then the word *años* (years).

English	Spanish
I'm six years old.	*Tengo seis años.*
I'm ten years old.	*Tengo diez años.*

Have a short conversation with a friend about ages. Here's a sample conversation:

ANA: *Hola, Carlos.*
CARLOS: *Buenos días.*

ANA: *¿Cuántos años tienes?*
CARLOS: *Tengo nueve años.*

ANA: *¡Yo también!*
CARLOS: *¡Qué interesante!*

ANA: *¡Hasta Luego!*
CARLOS: *¡Adiós, Ana!*

Now write your own conversation in the blank spaces provided and practice it with a friend:

SPEAKER 1: _____

SPEAKER 2: _____

SPEAKER 1: _____

SPEAKER 2: _____

Gramática —
Additional Grammar

To say that you are older than someone, use *mayor: Soy mayor que mi hermano* (I'm older than my brother). To say that you are younger, use *menor: Soy menor que mi prima* (I'm younger than my cousin).

SPEAKER 1: _____

SPEAKER 2: _____

SPEAKER 1: _____

SPEAKER 2: _____

Nice Party

Find your way from *el principio* (the start) to *el fin* (the end). Circle the number of *regalos de cumpleaños* you travel through.

UNO
DOS
TRES

el principio

el fin

CHAPTER 8

Food and Drink—
Comida y bebida

Be careful with the word *sopa*. It looks and sounds a lot like "soap," but it really means "soup." The last thing you want to do is ask for soup at the drugstore!

Meals and Courses—*Comidas y platos*

Eating new foods is one of the best things about traveling. If you go to Spain, Mexico, or another Spanish-speaking country, you'll definitely want to know how to talk about food. Here are some useful words to know:

English	Spanish
the meal	la comida
the breakfast	el desayuno
the lunch	el almuerzo
the dinner	la cena
the appetizer	el aperitivo
the soup	la sopa
the sandwich	el bocadillo, el sándwich
the main course	el plato principal
the salad	la ensalada
the dessert	el postre

Here is some general food vocabulary that you might find helpful:

English	Spanish
the bread	el pan
the French fries	las papas fritas
the jam	la mermelada
the mayonnaise	la mayonesa
the mustard	la mostaza
the oil	el aceite
the omelet	el omelette
the pepper	la pimienta
the rice	el arroz
the salt	la sal
the sugar	el azúcar
the toast	la tostada

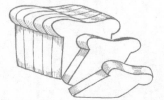

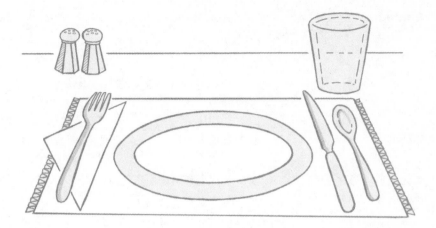

And here are some useful verbs related to eating and drinking.

English	Spanish
to be hungry	*tener hambre*
to eat	*comer*
to be thirsty	*tener sed*
to drink	*beber*

Gramática — Additional Grammar

The Spanish verb *tomar* is often used with food and drink. It means "to take," but you can use it to mean "eat" or "drink."

Fruit and Vegetables—*Frutas y vegetales*

Fruit and vegetables are good for you, but they taste good too! Here are the Spanish words for some delicious fruits:

English	Spanish
an apple	*una manzana*
an apricot	*un albaricoque*
a banana	*una banana, un banano*
a blackberry	*una mora*
a blueberry, cranberry	*un arándano*
a cherry	*una cereza*
a grape	*una uva*

English	Spanish
a grapefruit	*una toronja*
a lemon	*un limón*
a pineapple	*una piña*
a orange	*una naranja*
a peach	*un melocotón*
a pear	*una pera*
a plum	*una ciruela*
a raspberry	*una frambuesa*
a strawberry	*una fresa*

Don't forget the vegetables!

English	Spanish
the artichoke	*la alcachofa*
the asparagus	*el espárrago*
the beans	*los frijoles*
the carrot	*la zanahoria*
the celery	*el apio*
the corn	*el maíz*
the cucumber	*el pepino*
the eggplant	*la berenjena*
the garlic	*el ajo*
the lettuce	*la lechuga*
the mushroom	*el champiñón*
the olives	*las aceitunas*
the onion	*la cebolla*
the peas	*los guisantes*
the potato	*la papa, la patata*
the radish	*el rábano*
the spinach	*las espinacas*
the tomato	*el tomate*

Diversión—Fun Stuff

What are your favorite fruits and vegetables? Draw a garden with all of your favorites, and label them in Spanish. If you want to, you can use color, too. Use crayons or markers to draw the garden and then label the different fruits and vegetables with their names and colors. For example, for red strawberries, just write *fresas rojas*.

For a fun way to learn all the names of the different vegetables in Spanish, pretend you're making a big pot of soup.

What kind of soup would you like to make? What ingredients would you include? Fill in the following blank spaces with some of the veggies you'd like to put in your soup.

_____

_____

_____

_____

_____

Diversión_Fun Stuff

Draw a big picture of a pizza and then add a whole bunch of vegetable toppings. Don't forget to label all the veggies in Spanish! Some favorite combinations are spinach and mushroom, peppers and onions, or garlic and tomato. What are your favorites?

Meat and Dairy—*Carne y productos lácteos*

Here are some different kinds of meat and seafood. You'll want to know how to say all of these words in Spanish so you know what you're ordering when you go out to eat at a restaurant in a Spanish-speaking country.

English	Spanish
the tuna	*el atún*
the beef	*la carne de res*
the chicken	*el pollo*
the fish	*el pescado*
the ham	*el jamón*
the lamb	*el cordero*
the pork	*el cerdo*
the rabbit	*el conejo*
the roast beef	*el rosbif*
the sausage	*la salchicha*
the seafood	*el mariscos*
the steak	*el bistec*
the turkey	*el pavo*
the veal	*la ternera*

Consejo
IMPORTANT TIP

Do you remember learning that "fish" is *un pez* in the section on pets in Chapter 5? Well, *pez* is the word for a live fish, but when you talk about a fish that you're going to eat, it's called *pescado*.

LAS PAPAS FRITAS

LA SOPA

EL BOCADILLO

EL PAN

LA FRESA

LA LECHE

Let's Eat Lunch!

Find the picture suggested by each numbered clue and write the Spanish word into the puzzle grid. We left U-N-A P-I-Z-Z-A to help you out!

ACROSS

2 Slices of bread with a filling
5 _____ and crackers
6 Comes hot in a bowl or a cup
8 Autumn fruit of red or green
9 Drink made by a cow
12 Crispy hot potato strips
14 Summer fruit with many seeds
15 Comes in a loaf
16 You pour milk into this

DOWN

1 Summer citrus drink
3 Fruit in a bunch
4 Fruit served in a shortcake
6 Meat served on a bun with ketchup
7 Fruit with a small top and big bottom
10 Fruit with a long, yellow peel
11 Mix of green leaves and veggies
12 Sweet, baked treat eaten with milk
13 Crisp veggie stalk with a leafy top

LA SANDÍA

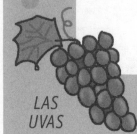

LAS UVAS

LA ENSALADA

EL APIO

EL PLÁTANO

LA HAMBURGUESA

LA LIMONADA

LA PERA

LA MANZANA

LA PERA

EL HELADO

EL HUEVO

LA GALLETA

EL VASO

EL QUESO

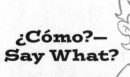

¿Cómo?— Say What?

An egg is *un huevo*. One dish you'll find in many Mexican restaurants is *huevos rancheros*, which are fried eggs with salsa. *Salsa*, by the way, just means "sauce" in Spanish, even though in English it refers only to the spicy tomato sauce you find in Mexican restaurants.

Here are some dairy products:

English	Spanish
the butter	*la mantequilla*
the buttermilk	*el suero de leche*
the cheese	*el queso*
the cream	*la crema*
the cottage cheese	*el requesón*
the ice cream	*el helado*
the milk	*la leche*
the yogurt	*el yogur*

Drinks and Desserts—*Bebidas y postres*

Now you just need a drink to go with all that great food! Here are some delicious drinks you might enjoy:

English	Spanish
the hot chocolate	*el chocolate*
the tea	*el té*
the iced tea	*el té helado*
the juice	*el jugo*
the lemonade	*la limonada*
the milk	*la leche*
the milkshake	*el batido*
the orange juice	*el jugo de naranja*
the smoothie	*el licuado (de frutas)*
the soda/pop	*el refresco*
the water	*el agua*

Consejo
IMPORTANT TIP

Ice is *el hielo* in Spanish. To ask for ice in your drink, say *con hielo*. If you don't want ice, say *sin hielo*. *Con* means "with" and *sin* means "without."

If you still have room after all of that great food, you can have some dessert. Here are some yummy choices:

English	Spanish
the cake	*el pastel, la torta*
the candy	*el dulce, las golosinas*
the chocolate	*el chocolate*
the cookie	*la galleta*
the jello	*la gelatina*
the donut	*la dona*
the fritter	*el buñuelo*
the fruit	*la fruta*
the ice cream	*el helado*
the muffin	*la magdalena*
the pie	*la tarta, el pastel*
the rice pudding	*el arroz con leche*
the vanilla	*la vainilla*

Consejo
IMPORTANT TIP

While Spanish speakers do enjoy the same desserts you do, like ice cream and cake, they also have some of their own favorites. Some desserts you might find in Spanish-speaking countries are *flan* (baked custard) and *plátanos al horno* (baked bananas).

I Like, I Don't Like—*Me gusta, no me gusta*

The verb or action word "to like" is an interesting verb in Spanish because it works a little differently than most verbs.

English	Spanish
I like	*Me gusta*
I don't like	*No me gusta*
He/she likes	*A ella/el le gusta*

Here are some examples with the verb *gustar*.

English	Spanish
I like ice cream.	*Me gusta el helado.*
I don't like cold showers.	*No me gustan las duchas frías.*
José likes to play soccer.	*A José le gusta jugar fútbol.*

Gramática —
Additional Grammar

If the thing or person you like is plural you need to add an *n* to *gusta*. You need to say *me gustan* or a *ella/el le gustan*.

Gramática —
Additional Grammar

Vegetarian is an adjective and just like all adjectives, it will change to agree with the gender and number of the noun it modifies. So if you're a girl, you'll say *Soy vegetariana*. If you're talking about more than one person, you would say *Somos vegetarianos* (We are vegetarians).

At the Restaurant—*En el restaurante*

When you go to a restaurant, you need to know more than just the names for food. You also need to be able to order what you want and maybe even explain that you can't eat certain things. This section will serve as your restaurant survival guide!

To order, you can either say *Me gustaría* or *Quisiera*. Both of these mean "I would like" and they are very polite. If you want to ask how much something costs, say *¿Cuánto cuesta . . . ?*

Here are some useful restaurant phrases:

English	Spanish
I can't eat . . .	*No puedo comer . . .*
I don't like . . .	*No me gusta . . .*
I'm allergic to . . .	*Tengo alergia a . . .*
I'm a vegetarian.	*Soy vegetariano.*
the menu	*el menú*
the check/bill	*la cuenta*
the tip	*la propina*
tip included	*servicio incluido*

Cooking in the Kitchen—*Cocinando en la cocina*

Now that you know the names of foods and drinks in Spanish, it is important that you learn the names of the pots and pans you use in the kitchen to cook your favorite foods. The kitchen has a lot of different things in it. How many of these can you find in your kitchen?

English	Spanish
a bottle	*una botella*
a bowl	*un tazón*

English	Spanish
a box	*una caja*
a can	*una lata*
a cookie sheet	*una bandeja de horno*
a cup	*una taza*
a dishwasher	*una lavavajillas*
a fork	*un tenedor*
a frying pan	*una sartén*
a glass	*un vaso*
a jar	*un pote*
a knife	*un cuchillo*
a napkin	*una servilleta*
an oven	*un horno*
a plate	*un plato*

Consejo
IMPORTANT TIP

Be careful about the word *vaso*, which means "glass." Don't let *vaso* fool you into thinking it means "vase"—that's called *un florero* in Spanish. These are false friends!

Hidden Foods

Can you find the five Spanish food words hidden in the following sentences? Look for words in the word list, but be careful—some words are not used!

WORD LIST
la fruta
la tarta
flan
la patata
el apio
la carne
la sal
el pepino
el pan

1. Food fight! Splat art! Annoy mom!
2. In a tunnel, a car never goes fast.
3. A morsel, Pa. Not a lot!
4. I eat food of land and sea.
5. I will fill a salad bowl.

English	Spanish
a pot	*una olla*
a refrigerator	*un refrigerador, una nevera*
a saucer	*un platillo*
a sink	*un fregadero*
a spatula	*una espátula*
a spoon	*una cuchara*
a stove	*una estufa, una cocina*
a whisk	*un batidor*
a wooden spoon	*una cuchara de madera*

Now see if you can remember what all these kitchen words mean! Use the following checklist to find all these items in your kitchen. As you find each one, write a checkmark in the box next to it. You'll have to recognize the Spanish words, so this may be a little tricky!

- ❑ *un tenedor*
- ❑ *un tazón*
- ❑ *una lata*
- ❑ *una taza*
- ❑ *una sartén*
- ❑ *un fregadero*
- ❑ *un pote*
- ❑ *un cuchillo*
- ❑ *un plato*
- ❑ *una cuchara*

Luisa and Pedro are very good friends and they decided to cook a nice dinner.

Gramática —
Additional Grammar

In Spanish, the word ending *-illo* means little. So *un plato* is a plate, and *un platillo* is a little plate—or a saucer!

CHAPTER 9

Who Are You?—
¿Quién eres?

¿Dónde vives?

Where Do You Live?—¿Dónde vives?

When you travel or meet people, one of the first things you will probably talk about is where you live.

To ask where someone lives, say *¿Dónde vives?*

The answer begins with *Vivo en* (I live in), followed by a city, state, province, or country.

English	Spanish
Where do you live?	*¿Dónde vives?*
I live in Detroit.	*Vivo en Detroit.*
I live in California.	*Vivo en California.*
I live in Canada.	*Vivo en Canadá.*
I live near Los Angeles.	*Vivo cerca de Los Angeles.*
I live near Chicago.	*Vivo cerca de Chicago.*

To ask where someone is from (which might not be the same as where he or she lives now), ask *¿De dónde eres?* And then you can answer *Soy de* (I'm from) or *Nací en* (I was born in).

English	Spanish
Where are you from?	*¿De dónde eres?*
I'm from Houston.	*Soy de Houston.*
I'm from Ontario.	*Soy de Ontario.*
I was born in Portland.	*Nací en Portland.*
I was born in New York.	*Nací en Nueva York.*

You might also want to say that you used to live somewhere:

English	Spanish
I used to live in San Francisco.	*Vivía en San Francisco.*
I used to live in Florida.	*Vivía en La Florida.*

¿Cómo?— Say What?

If you live in a small town that people in other countries have never heard of, you might like to say *Vivo cerca de* (I live near) and then the nearest city.

And finally, if you want to keep in touch with someone, you'll need to give them your address or phone number.

English	Spanish	
My address is	*Mi dirección es*	_____
My e-mail address is	*Mi dirección electrónica es*	_____
My phone number is	*Mi número de teléfono es*	_____

Countries—*Países*

Knowing the Spanish words for different countries will be useful in many ways: for talking about where you are from and where you are traveling to, as well as for understanding where the people you meet are from.

Many places have the same name in Spanish and English:

- Argentina
- Australia
- Guatemala
- Chile
- Perú
- Colombia
- Costa Rica
- Ecuador
- Bolivia
- Puerto Rico
- Cuba

Gramática — Additional Grammar

Like all other vocabulary, the Spanish words for countries have gender. If the word ends in *a*, it's feminine: *la Colombia, la Costa Rica*. Otherwise, it's masculine: *el Ecuador, el México*. Now, you will not use *el* or *la* when talking about the country by itself. So to say "Costa Rica is a beautiful country," you would omit *la* and just say *Costa Rica es un país muy bello*. You would use *el* or *la* when you are talking about certain characteristics of the country; for example, to say "A common food in ancient Mexico was corn," you would say *El maíz era una comida común en el México antiguo*.

Here are a couple of sample sentences to guide you:

English	Spanish
I want to go to Australia.	*Quiero ir a Australia.*
I went to Costa Rica last year.	*Fui a Costa Rica el año pasado.*

Consejo
IMPORTANT TIP

Just as United States has the abbreviation U.S., *los Estados Unidos* is abbreviated to los EE. UU.

But for others, the words are different in Spanish and English.

English	Spanish	English	Spanish
Africa	*África*	Japan	*Japón*
Brazil	*Brasil*	Mexico	*México*
Canada	*Canadá*	Panama	*Panamá*
Egypt	*Egipto*	Poland	*Polonia*
England	*Inglaterra*	Russia	*Rusia*
Europe	*Europa*	Spain	*España*
France	*Francia*	Switzerland	*Suiza*
Germany	*Alemania*	United States	*Estados Unidos*
Italy	*Italia*		

Nationality—*Nacionalidad*

Another way to talk about where you're from is to talk about your nationality. For example, if you are from America, you are American. Here are some other nationalities in the world:

English	Spanish
African	*africano*
American (United States)	*estadounidense*
American (North or South)	*americano*
Argentine	*argentino*
Asian	*asiático*
Australian	*australiano*
Brazilian	*brasileño*
Canadian	*canadiense*
Chilean	*chileno*
Chinese	*chino*
Colombian	*colombiano*
Costa Rican	*costarricense*
Ecuadorian	*ecuatoriano*

English	Spanish
Egyptian	*egipcio*
English	*inglés*
European	*europeo*
French	*francés*
German	*alemán*
Indian	*indio*
Italian	*italiano*
Japanese	*japonés*
Mexican	*mexicano*
Polish	*polaco*
Portuguese	*portugués*
Puerto Rican	*puertorriqueño*
Russian	*ruso*
Spanish	*español*
Swiss	*suizo*

English	Spanish
I am American.	*Soy estadounidense.*
My mom is a Spaniard.	*Mi madre es española.*

Languages—*Idiomas*

There are hundreds of languages in the world. Here are the Spanish names for the ones you might need to talk about.

English	Spanish
Arabic	*el árabe*
Catalan	*el catalán*
Chinese	*el chino*
Dutch	*el holandés*
English	*el inglés*
French	*el francés*

¡CUIDADO!
Mistake to Avoid

In Spanish, all languages are masculine and are not capitalized. The same is true for nationalities. For example: "the Spanish language" would be *el idioma español*, and "He is a Spaniard" would be *Él es español.*

101

¿Cómo?– Say What?

The Spanish spoken in Spain is known as Castilian Spanish. It is different from the Spanish spoken in Latin America, just as the English spoken in the United States is different from English in England.

English	Spanish
German	el alemán
Italian	el italiano
Japanese	el japonés
Korean	el coreano
Persian	el persa
Polish	el polaco
Portuguese	el portugués
Russian	el ruso
Spanish	el español
Vietnamese	el vietnamita

English	Spanish
I speak English and Spanish.	Hablo inglés y español.
I don't speak German.	No hablo alemán.

Do you know anyone who speaks a second language? Perhaps one of your parents learned another language in college, or you have a friend from a different country. For some more writing practice, write down some sentences explaining who of your friends and family speaks another language. Remember that the words for different languages are lowercased when written in Spanish. Here are a couple of examples:

English	Spanish
My mother speaks Italian.	Mi madre habla italiano.
My friend speaks French.	Mi amigo habla francés.

Now try writing your own sentences in the spaces below:

Hablo inglés.

When I Grow Up—*Cuando sea grande*

What do you want to be when you grow up? What do you want to do, where do you want to live? This section will help you talk about all of your dreams for the future.

English	Spanish
I want to be . . .	*Quiero ser . . .*
I want to be a fireman.	*Quiero ser bombero.*
I want to be a doctor.	*Quiero ser médico.*
I'm going to be . . .	*Voy a ser . . .*
I'm going to be an artist.	*Voy a ser artista.*
I'm going to be a teacher.	*Voy a ser profesor.*
I don't want to be . . .	*No quiero ser . . .*
I don't want to be a writer.	No *quiero ser escritor.*
I don't want to be a manager.	*No quiero ser gerente.*
I want to live in . . .	*Quiero vivir en . . .*
I want to live in Spain.	*Quiero vivir en España.*
I want to live in Buenos Aires.	*Quiero vivir en Buenos Aires.*
I don't want to live in . . .	*No quiero vivir en . . .*
I don't want to live in the U.S.	*No quiero vivir en los EE. UU.*
I don't want to live in Miami	*No quiero vivir en Miami.*
I dream of . . .	*Mi sueño es . . .*
I dream of traveling around Spain.	*Mi sueño es viajar por España.*
I dream of being president.	*Mi sueño es ser presidente.*

Gramática — Additional Grammar

To ask someone else about his or her dreams, use *¿Qué quieres?* (What do you want) or *¿Dónde quieres ?* (Where do you want) followed by *ir* (to go), *vivir* (to live), or *ser* (to be). *¿Qué quieres ser?* (What do you want to be?) *¿Dónde quieres vivir?* (Where do you want to live?)

CHAPTER 10

Just for Fun—*Sólo para diversión*

Sports—*Deportes*

Well, you've made it through nine chapters, learning the vocabulary you need to talk about what you have to do. Now you can finally learn how to talk about what you do to have fun!

If you like to play sports, here is the Spanish for the most common ones. For all of these, you can say *Me gusta* (I like) or *No me gusta* (I don't like). You can also say *Juego* (I play) and *Miro* (I watch).

English	Spanish
baseball	*el béisbol*
basketball	*el baloncesto*
football	*el fútbol americano*
golf	*el golf*
hockey	*el hockey*
rugby	*el rugby*
soccer	*el fútbol*
tennis	*el tenis*
volleyball	*el voleibol*

For example:

English	Spanish
I like baseball.	*Me gusta el béisbol.*
I don't like tennis.	*No me gusta el tenis.*
I play soccer.	*Juego fútbol.*

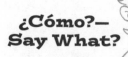

¿Cómo?— Say What?

There are a few different variations on skiing and skating in both English and Spanish. In Spanish, water-skiing is *el esquí acuático*, while cross-country skiing is *el esquí de fondo*. Ice skating is *el patinaje sobre hielo* and roller skating is *el patinaje sobre ruedas*.

For a few sports you can't use *juego* because you don't play them. Instead, you use the verb for "doing" the sport. But you can still use *Me gusta*, *No me gusta*, and *Miro*. Here are some sports that use the action verb instead of "play" as well as examples of *Me gusta* and *Miro*.

English	Spanish
boxing	*el boxeo*
skating	*el patinaje*
skiing	*el esquí*
wrestling	*la lucha*

For example:

English	Spanish
I box.	*Yo boxeo.*
I like skating.	*Me gusta el patinaje.*
I watch wrestling.	*Miro la lucha.*

Games—*Juegos*

For games, you can use the same verbs as for sports: *Juego*, *Me gusta*, and *No me gusta*. Here are some games you might like to play with friends and family:

un juego de cartas

English	Spanish
a board game	un juego de tablero
backgammon	el backgammon
checkers	las damas
chess	el ajedrez
Chinese checkers	las damas chinas
dominoes	el dominó
monopoly	el monopolio
card game	un juego de cartas/de naipes/de barajas
bridge	el bridge
gin rummy	el gin rummy
hearts	los corazones
poker	el póquer
rummy	el rummy
solitaire	el solitario

The suits in the Spanish cards are *oros* (gold pieces), *espadas* (swords), *copas* (cups), and *bastos* (clubs). They are very colorful and you can play games you've never even heard of before.

Here are some sample sentences:

English	Spanish
I play chess.	Juego ajedrez.
I like dominoes.	Me gusta el dominó.
I don't like solitaire.	No me gusta el solitario.

Consejo
IMPORTANT TIP

In Spanish-speaking countries, there are two different decks of cards. The traditional cards you know and play with in the United States are known in Spanish as *barajas francesas* (French cards) and also there is a special deck of Spanish cards called *naipes españoles* that has different suits and drawings. The four suits in the traditional cards are called *corazones* (hearts), *diamantes* (diamonds), *picas* (spades), and *tréboles* (clubs). You already know all the numbers, but you might need help with the face cards: *as* (ace), *sota* (jack), *reina* (queen), and *rey* (king). And don't forget the joker: ¡*el comodín*!

I Win!

Use the decoder to find a Spanish word to answer the riddle. What does this word mean? Add the numbers used in the answer and check the key!

=A

=D

=L

=M

=S

What familiar game is played with a lot of jumping?

____ ____ ____   ____ ____ ____ ____ ____

KEY: | 20 JUMP ROPE | 21 HOPSCOTCH | 22 CHECKERS |

Here are some other games you might enjoy:

English	Spanish
the darts	*los dardos*
the pinball machine	*la máquina de pinball*
the ping pong	*el tenis de mesa, el ping-pong*
the pool	*el billar*
a videogame	*un videojuego*

What do you like to play? Make a list of the games you like the most using the blank spaces below.

_____

_____

_____

_____

Gramática —
Additional Grammar

When you say that you want to get on a ride you need to use the verb *subirse*. To say "I am going to get on the ferris wheel" you say *Voy a subirme a la rueda de Chicago.* If you actually prefer to get off you use the verb *bajarse* and you would say *Voy a bajarme de la rueda de Chicago.* Of course you need to wait until it stops before doing something like that. You get the idea! You also use *subirse* and *bajarse* to get on and off a bus, a bike, a train, etc.

Now compare the games you like with the games your friends like. To ask a friend what he or she likes to play, ask, *¿Qué te gusta jugar?*

Amusement Park—*Parque de diversiones*

Amusement parks are great places for the whole family because they have a lot of different things that can be enjoyed at any age. Next time you go to one, you can say the word in Spanish for some of the rides and activities. Here are some of those words:

English	Spanish
the roller coaster	*la montaña rusa*
the bumper cars	*los carros chocones*
the merry-go-round	*el carrusel*
the ferris wheel	*la rueda de Chicago*
the pirate ship	*el barco pirata*
the castle	*el castillo*
the parade	*el desfile*
the cotton candy	*el algodón de azúcar*
a drink	*una bebida*
the ride	*el juego mecánico*
the show	*el espectáculo*
to be dizzy	*estar mareado*
to be scared	*estar asustado*
to have fun	*divertirse*
to spin	*girar*
to wait in line	*hacer fila*

Here are some sample sentences:

English	Spanish
Let's go to an amusement park.	*Vamos a un parque de diversiones.*
I like that roller coaster.	*Me gusta esa montaña rusa.*
We have to wait in line.	*Tenemos que hacer fila.*
I want cotton candy.	*Quiero algodón de azúcar.*

Write down what you enjoy the most and the least when you go to *un parque de diversiones*:

Me gusta _____ *y* _____ .

No me gusta _____ .

Quiero beber _____ .

Gramática — Additional Grammar

Talking about hunting and fishing is different than talking about most activities, which need the verb *Hago* (I do). For hunting and fishing, you use *Voy* (I go) instead: *Voy de caza* (I go hunting) and *Voy de pesca* (I go fishing).

Activities—*Actividades*

Here are some other kinds of outside activities that you might enjoy with your friends and family:

English	Spanish
biking	*el ciclismo*
fishing	*la pesca*
gardening	*la jardinería*
hiking	*el senderismo*
hunting	*la caza*
jogging	*trotar*
running	*correr*
sailing	*la navegación a vela*
skateboarding	*el monopatinaje*
swimming	*la natación*

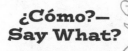

¿Cómo?— Say What?

What do you like to collect? How about dolls (*muñecas*), stamps (*estampillas*), rubber stamps (*sellos de goma*), coins (*monedas*), comic books (*historietas*), marbles (*canicas*), or toy cars (*automóviles de juguete*)?

And some indoor activities:

English	Spanish
collecting	el coleccionismo
cooking	la cocina
jigsaw puzzle	el rompecabezas
juggling	el malabarismo
magic	la magia
reading	la lectura
writing	la escritura

Here are some sample sentences:

English	Spanish
I like cooking.	Me gusta la cocina.
I don't like juggling.	No me gusta el malabarismo.

TV and Movies—*Televisión y películas*

Watching movies and television can be fun, and they can also teach you all about people, places, and things. Here are some Spanish words relating to movies:

English	Spanish
a movie	una película
a movie theater	un cine
an action movie	una película de acción
a classic movie	una película clásica
a comedy	una comedia
a documentary	un documental
a drama	un drama
a horror movie	una película de terror
a romance movie	una película romántica
a romantic comedy	una comedia romántica

Here are some words to use when talking about television:

English	Spanish
the television	*la televisión*
cartoons	*dibujos animados*
a miniseries	*una miniserie*
a sitcom	*una comedia de situación*
a soap opera	*una telenovela*
a TV show	*un programa de televisión*
a TV station	*una estación de televisión*
a TV network	*una cadena de televisión*

Ask your parents if you can rent a Spanish movie and watch it together. This is a great way to see how much Spanish you've actually learned. When the movie is over, talk about what kind of movie it was, what you liked about it, and what you didn't like about it.

Music and Dance—*Música y baile*

Do you like music? Of course you do! But what kind of music do you like? Here are some words to help you chat about music:

English	Spanish
the music	*la música*
the blues	*el blues*
classical music	*la música clásica*
country music	*la música country*
folk music	*la música folklórica*
heavy metal	*el rock pesado*
jazz	*el jazz*
rap	*el rap*
rock and roll	*el rock and roll*

With music, you can use *Me gusta* and *No me gusta* again. For example:

English	Spanish
I like classical music.	*Me gusta la música clásica.*
I don't like jazz.	*No me gusta el jazz.*

¡CUIDADO!
Mistake to Avoid

Be careful—*programa* ends in *a*, but it's masculine. For example: *Es un nuevo programa* means "It's a new program."

Gramática —
Additional Grammar

Another verb you can use is *Escucho* (I listen to): *Escucho el rap*—"I listen to rap (music)." *No escucho el rock and roll*—"I don't listen to rock and roll." And if you sing, you need the verb *cantar*. To say "I sing," say *Canto*.

Consejo
IMPORTANT TIP

There are many different types of music and dance from the Spanish-speaking world: tango from Argentina, flamenco from Spain, mambo and rumba from Cuba, merengue from the Dominican Republic, and mariachi from Mexico. Have you heard of any of these?

Or maybe you like to play music. Here are some instruments:

English	Spanish
the drum	*el tambor*
the flute	*la flauta*
the guitar	*la guitarra*
the piano	*el piano*
the saxophone	*el saxofón*
the trumpet	*la trompeta*
the violin	*el violin*

To play an instrument, use *Toco*:

English	Spanish
I play the violin.	*Toco el violín.*
I play the flute.	*Toco la flauta.*

Do you like to dance? Here are some kinds of dance and some other words to use with them.

English	Spanish
dancing	*el baile*
ballet	*el ballet*
ballroom dancing	*el baile de salón*
hip hop	*el hip hop*
jazz	*el jazz*
modern	*el baile moderno*
tap dance	*el tap*

Nifty Knitter

While this girl practices her *labor de punto* (knitting), you can match the six words that are sounded out to the correct words in the word list. Then look for these items hidden in the picture!

WORD SOUNDS
1. el poy-oh
2. el dya-man-teh
3. el cor-ah-sewn
4. la yah-bay
5. la coh-meh-ta
6. el goo-san-oh

WORD LIST
___ el **corazón** *heart*
___ el **pollo** *chicken*
___ el **gusano** *worm*
___ el **diamante** *diamond*
___ la **llave** *key*
___ la **cometa** *kite*

¿Cómo?— Say What?

Art projects like knitting and needlepoint are done with yarn and string. In Spanish, both of these materials are called *el hilo*, but yarn can also be called *el hilo de lana*. If you need a needle, that's *una aguja*.

Arts and Crafts—*Arte y manualidades*

If you're the artistic type, you'll probably find some of this vocabulary helpful.

English	Spanish
crocheting	*tejer a crochet*
embroidery	*el bordado*
knitting	*tejer*
macrame	*el macramé*
needlepoint	*el medio punto*
quilting	*hacer edredones*
sewing	*coser*
weaving	*tejer*
basketry	*la cestería*
collage	*el collage*
drawing	*dibujar*
painting	*pintar*
photography	*la fotografía*
pottery	*la alfarería*
rubber stamps	*los sellos de goma*
sculpture	*la escultura*
scrapbook	*el álbum de recortes*
woodworking	*la ebanistería*

If you could do whatever you wanted every day, would you just play the same game all the time, or would you play soccer on Monday and paint on Tuesday? Use the following spaces to write up your dream schedule—in Spanish, of course!

lunes	*martes*	*miércoles*	*jueves*	*viernes*	*sábado*	*domingo*

English-Spanish Glossary

English	Spanish
an accent	*un acento*
an action movie	*una película de acción*
an actor/actress	*un actor, una actriz*
an adding machine	*una sumadora*
Africa	*África*
African	*un africano, una africana*
the airport	*el aeropuerto*
an alarm clock	*un despertador*
the almonds	*las almendras*
American (North + South)	*un americano, una americana*
American (United States)	*un/una estadounidense*
and	*y*
And you?	*¿Y tú?*
angry	*enojado*
the ankle	*el tobillo*
annoyed	*enfadado*
an ant	*una hormiga*
the appetizer	*el aperitivo*
an apple	*una manzana*
an apricot	*un albaricoque*
April	*abril*
Arabic	*el árabe*
an arch	*un arco*
Argentine	*argentino/a*
the arm	*el brazo*
Arrivals	*Llegadas*
the art	*el arte*
the artichoke	*la alcachofa*
an artist	*un/una artista*
Asian	*asiático/a*
the asparagus	*el espárrago*
athletic	*atlético/a*

English	Spanish
the attic	*el ático*
August	*agosto*
the aunt	*la tía*
Australian	*australiano/a*
the autumn	*el otoño*
a baby	*un/una bebé*
the back	*la espalda*
backgammon	*el backgammon*
a backpack	*una mochila*
the baggage	*el equipaje*
the baggage claim	*el reclamo de equipaje*
a baker	*un panadero, una panadera*
the bakery	*la panadería*
the balcony	*el balcón*
ballet	*el ballet*
ballroom dancing	*el baile de salón*
a banana	*una banana, un banano*
the bank	*el banco*
the barber	*la barbería*
baseball	*el béisbol*
the basement	*el sótano*
basketball	*el baloncesto*
basketry	*la cestería*
a bathing suit	*un traje de baño*
the bathroom	*el baño*
a bathtub	*una bañera, un baño*
the beans	*los frijoles*
the beauty shop	*la peluquería*
a bed	*una cama*
the bedroom	*el dormitorio*
the beef	*la carne de res*
the beer	*la cerveza*
a belt	*un cinturón*
the bicycle	*la bicicleta*

English	Spanish
big	*grande*
biking	*el ciclismo*
a bikini	*un biquini*
biology	*biología*
a bird	*un pájaro*
the birthday	*el cumpleaños*
a birthday cake	*una torta, un pastel de cumpleaños*
a birthday card	*una tarjeta de cumpleaños*
a birthday party	*una fiesta de cumpleaños*
a birthday present	*un regalo de cumpleaños*
black	*negro*
black hair	*el cabello negro, el pelo negro*
a blackberry	*una mora*
a blizzard	*una ventisca*
blond hair	*el cabello rubio, el pelo rubio*
a blouse	*una blusa*
blue	*azul*
a blueberry	*un arándano*
the blues	*los blues*
a board game	*un juego de tablero*
the boarding pass	*la tarjeta de embarque*
the boat	*el barco*
a book	*un libro*
a bookshelf	*una estantería*
the bookstore	*la librería*
some boots	*unas botas*
bored	*aburrido/a*
boring	*aburrido/a*
a bottle	*una botella*
a bowl	*un tazón*
a box	*una caja*
some boxer shorts	*unos calzoncillos*
boxing	*el boxeo*
a boy	*un niño, un chico*
a boyfriend	*un novio*
a bra	*un sostén*
a bracelet	*un brazalete*
brave	*valiente*
Brazil	*Brasil*
Brazilian	*brasileño*
the bread	*el pan*

English	Spanish
breakfast	*el desayuno*
the bridge	*el bridge*
a briefcase	*un maletín*
the brother	*el hermano*
brown	*marrón*
brown hair	*el cabello castaño, el pelo castaño*
the bus	*el autobús*
the butcher shop	*la carnicería*
the butter	*la mantequilla*
the buttermilk	*el suero de leche*
bye	*chao*
bye-bye	*chaíto*
the cake	*la torta, el pastel*
a calculator	*una calculadora*
a can	*una lata*
Canada	*Canadá*
Canadian	*canadiense*
candy	*el dulce, las golosinas*
the candy store	*la confitería*
the car	*el automóvil*
a card game	*un juego de cartas*
a carpenter	*un carpintero, una carpintera*
a carpet	*una alfombra*
the carrot	*la zanahoria*
the carry-on luggage	*el equipaje de mano*
cartoons	*dibujos animados*
the cashews	*las semillas de marañón*
a cashier	*un cajero, una cajera*
a cat	*un gato, una gata*
Catalan	*catalán*
Catch you later!	*¡Nos vemos!*
CD-ROM	*un CD-ROM*
the ceiling	*el techo*
the celery	*el apio*
a chair	*una silla*
a chalk	*una tiza*
a chalkboard	*una pizarra*
the check, bill	*la cuenta*
checkers	*las damas*
the check-in desk	*el mostrador de registro*
the cheek	*la mejilla*
the cheese	*el queso*

English	Spanish	English	Spanish
chemistry	*química*	the cream	*la crema*
a cherry	*una cereza*	a crescent	*una media luna*
chess	*el ajedrez*	crocheting	*tejer a crochet*
the chest	*el pecho*	a cube	*un cubo*
the chicken	*el pollo*	the cucumber	*el pepino*
Chilean	*chileno/a*	a cup	*una taza*
Chinese	*chino/a*	the curly hair	*el cabello rizado, el pelo rizado*
Chinese checkers	*las damas chinas*	the currency exchange	*el cambio de moneda*
chocolate	*el chocolate*	a curtain	*una cortina*
Christmas	*la Navidad*	a curve	*una curva*
Christmas Eve	*la Nochebuena*	customs	*la aduana*
a circle	*un círculo*	a cylinder	*un cilindro*
civics	*educación cívica*	dancing	*el baile*
a class	*una clase*	the dark hair	*el cabello oscuro, el pelo oscuro*
classic movie	*una película clásica*	dark purple	*morado*
classical music	*la música clásica*	dark red	*rojo oscuro*
a classmate	*un compañero, una compañera*	the darts	*los dardos*
a classroom	*una aula*	a database	*una base de datos*
a closet	*un clóset*	the daughter	*la hija*
the clothing store	*la tienda de ropa*	December	*diciembre*
a coat	*un abrigo*	the den	*el estudio*
coffee	*el café*	the dentist	*el/la dentista*
cold	*frío*	the department store	*la tienda por departamentos*
collage	*el collage*	Departures	*Salidas*
collecting	*el coleccionismo*	depressed	*deprimido/a*
a college	*una universidad*	a desk	*un escritorio*
Colombian	*colombiano/a*	the dessert	*el postre*
a comedy	*una comedia*	a diamond	*un diamante*
a computer	*una computadora*	a dictionary	*un diccionario*
a cone	*un cono*	the dining room	*el comedor*
a cook	*un cocinero, una cocinera*	dinner	*la cena*
the cookie	*la galleta*	a dishwasher	*una lavavajillas*
a cookie sheet	*una bandeja de horno*	a disk drive	*una unidad de disco*
cooking	*la cocina*	dizzy	*mareado*
a copy machine	*una copiadora*	a doctor	*un doctor, una doctora*
the corn	*el maíz*	a documentary	*un documental*
Costa Rican	*costarricense*	a dog	*un perro, una perra*
the cottage cheese	*el requesón*	the doghouse	*la caseta del perro*
a couch	*un canapé*	dominoes	*el dominó*
country music	*la música country*	don't mention it	*no hay de qué*
the cousin	*el primo, la prima*	the donut	*la dona*
crayons	*lápices de color*	a door	*una puerta*

English	Spanish	English	Spanish
down	*abajo*	excuse me	*con permiso*
Dr.	*Doctor*	the eye	*el ojo*
a drama	*un drama*	the eye doctor	*el optometrista*
the drawing	*el dibujo*	the face	*la cara*
a dress	*un vestido*	far	*lejos*
a dresser	*un tocador*	fat	*gordo/a*
a driver	*un conductor*	Father's Day	*el Día del Padre*
the driveway	*la entrada del automóvil*	a fax machine	*una máquina de fax*
a drought	*una sequía*	fear	*miedo*
the drum	*el tambor*	February	*febrero*
the dry cleaner	*la tintorería*	the fence	*la valla*
a dryer	*una secadora*	a ferret	*un hurón*
Dutch	*holandés*	the ferry	*el transbordador*
the duty-free store	*la tienda libre de impuestos*	fifteen	*quince*
the ear	*la oreja*	fifty	*cincuenta*
some earrings	*unos aretes*	a file	*un archivo*
east	*este*	a file folder	*una carpeta*
Easter	*la Pascua*	a filing cabinet	*un archivador*
economy (coach) class	*la clase económica*	the finger	*el dedo*
Ecuadorian	*ecuatoriano/a*	the fingernail	*la uña*
the eggplant	*la berenjena*	a fireman	*un bombero, una bombera*
Egypt	*Egipto*	first class	*la primera clase*
Egyptian	*egipcio/a*	a fish	*un pez*
eight	*ocho*	the fish (to eat)	*el pescado*
eighteen	*dieciocho*	fishing	*la pesca*
eighty	*ochenta*	five	*cinco*
the elbow	*el codo*	a flight	*un vuelo*
an electrician	*un/una electricista*	a flight attendant	*un/una auxiliar de vuelo*
eleven	*once*	a flood	*una inundación*
the e-mail	*el correo electrónico*	the floor	*el piso*
the e-mail address	*la dirección electrónica*	the flower	*la flor*
embarrassed	*avergonzado*	the flute	*la flauta*
embroidery	*el bordado*	folk music	*la música folklórica*
an employee	*un empleado, una empleada*	the foot	*el pie*
an engineer	*un ingeniero, una ingeniera*	football	*el fútbol americano*
England	*Inglaterra*	forgive me	*perdóneme, discúlpeme*
English	*inglés*	a fork	*un tenedor*
an eraser	*un borrador*	forty	*cuarenta*
the espresso	*el café expreso*	four	*cuatro*
Europe	*Europa*	fourteen	*catorce*
European	*europeo/a*	France	*Francia*
excited	*entusiasmado/a*	French	*francés*

English	Spanish
the French fries	*las papas fritas*
Friday	*viernes*
a friend	*un amigo, una amiga*
friendly	*amistoso*
the fritter	*el buñuelo*
a frog	*una rana*
the fruit	*la fruta*
the fruit stand	*la frutería*
a frying pan	*una sartén*
funny	*divertido*
the garage	*el garaje*
the garden	*el jardín*
gardening	*la jardinería*
the garlic	*el ajo*
the gate	*el portón*
a gate (at airport)	*una puerta de embarque*
geography	*geografía*
the gerbil	*un gerbo*
German	*alemán*
Germany	*Alemania*
gin rummy	*el gin rummy*
a girl	*una niña, una chica, una muchacha*
a girlfriend	*una novia*
a glass	*un vaso*
a glasses	*unas gafas*
a gloves	*unos guantes*
the glue	*la goma*
golf	*el golf*
Good afternoon	*Buenas tardes*
Good evening	*Buenas noches*
Good night	*Buenas noches*
Goodbye	*Adiós*
good-looking	*guapo, guapa*
the granddaughter	*la nieta*
the grandfather	*el abuelo*
the grandmother	*la abuela*
the grandson	*el nieto*
a grape	*una uva*
a grapefruit	*una toronja*
gray	*gris*
green	*verde*
the grocery store	*la tienda de comestibles*

English	Spanish
a guinea pig	*un cobayo*
the guitar	*la guitarra*
gym, physical education	*educación física*
the hair	*el cabello, el pelo*
the hall	*el pasillo*
the ham	*el jamón*
the hammock	*la hamaca*
a hamster	*un hámster*
the hand	*la mano*
happy	*feliz, alegre*
Happy birthday!	*¡Feliz cumpleaños!*
a hard drive	*un disco duro*
the hardware	*el hardware*
the hardware store	*la ferretería*
a hat	*un sombrero*
Have a nice day	*Que tenga(s) un buen día*
He is . . .	*Él es . . .*
the head	*la cabeza*
a heart	*un corazón*
the hearts	*los corazones*
heavy metal	*el rock pesado*
the helicopter	*el helicóptero*
Hello	*Hola*
Her name is . . .	*Ella se llama . . .*
a hermit crab	*un cangrejo ermitaño*
a hexagon	*un hexágono*
Hi	*Hola*
a high school	*un colegio*
some high-heeled shoes	*unos zapatos de tacones altos*
a highlighter	*un marcador*
hiking	*el senderismo*
hip hop	*el hip hop*
His name is . . .	*Él se llama . . .*
history	*historia*
hockey	*el hockey*
home economics	*economía doméstica*
the homework	*la tarea*
a horror movie	*una película de terror*
a horse	*un caballo*
the hose	*la manga*
the hospital	*el hospital*
the hot chocolate	*el chocolate caliente*

English	Spanish	English	Spanish
the hotel	*el hotel*	Italian	*el italiano*
how	*cómo*	Italy	*Italia*
How are you?	*¿Cómo está(s)?*	itchy	*comezón*
How do you say in Spanish?	*¿Cómo se dice en español?*	It's bad weather	*Hace mal tiempo*
		It's cloudy	*Está nublado*
How do you spell ?	*¿Cómo se escribe ?*	It's cold	*Hace frío*
how much?	*¿cúanto?*	It's cool	*Está fresco*
How's it going?	*¿Qué tal?*	It's foggy	*Hay neblina*
huge	*enorme*	It's hot	*Hace calor*
hunting	*la caza*	It's nice out	*Hace buen tiempo*
a hurricane	*un huracán*	It's nice to meet you	*Mucho gusto*
the husband	*el esposo*	It's sunny	*Hay sol, está soleado*
I can't eat . . .	*No puedo comer . . .*	It's windy	*Hace viento*
I don't know	*No sé*	It is . . .	*Está . . .*
I don't like . . .	*No me gusta . . .*	a jacket	*una chaqueta*
I have a question	*Tengo una pregunta*	jam	*la mermelada*
I live in . . .	*Vivo en . . .*	January	*enero*
I live near . . .	*Vivo cerca de . . .*	Japan	*Japón*
I thank you	*Te lo agradezco*	Japanese	*el japonés*
I want . . .	*Quiero, Deseo . . .*	a jar	*un pote*
I was born in . . .	*Nací en . . .*	jazz dance	*el jazz-ballet*
I would like . . .	*Quisiera . . .*	jazz music	*el jazz*
the ice cream	*el helado*	jealous	*celoso*
the iced tea	*el té helado*	the jello	*la gelatina*
I'm a vegetarian	*Soy vegetariano, soy vegetariana*	the jet ski	*la moto acuática*
I'm allergic to . . .	*Tengo alergia a . . .*	the jigsaw puzzle	*el rompecabezas*
I'm from . . .	*Soy de . . .*	jogging	*trotar*
I'm going . . .	*Yo voy . . .*	Judaism	*el judaísmo*
I'm good	*(Estoy) bien*	juggling	*el malabarismo*
I'm great	*(Estoy) muy bien*	the juice	*el jugo*
I'm sorry	*Lo siento*	July	*julio*
I'm very sorry	*Lo siento mucho*	June	*junio*
immigration	*la inmigración*	a keyboard	*un teclado*
impatient	*impaciente*	kind	*amable*
in back of	*detrás de*	the kitchen	*la cocina*
in front of	*enfrente de*	the knee	*la rodilla*
an index card	*una ficha*	a knife	*un cuchillo*
Indian	*indio*	knitting	*tejer*
interesting	*interesante*	Korean	*coreano*
Internet	*el Internet*	the lamb	*el cordero*
an Internet browser	*un motor de búsqueda*	a lamp	*una lámpara*
a Internet café	*un café Internet*	a laptop (computer)	*una computadora portátil*

English-Spanish Glossary

English	Spanish	English	Spanish
large	*grande*	the milk	*la leche*
Latin	*latín*	the milkshake	*el batido*
the laundromat	*la lavandería*	a miniseries	*una miniserie*
a lawyer	*un abogado, una abogada*	a mirror	*un espejo*
a layover	*una escala*	Miss	*Señorita*
lazy	*perezoso/a*	some mittens	*unos mitones*
left	*a la izquierda*	modern dance	*el baile moderno*
the leg	*la pierna*	Monday	*lunes*
a lemon	*un limón*	a monitor	*un monitor*
the lemonade	*la limonada*	Monopoly	*el Monopolio*
the lettuce	*la lechuga*	Mother's Day	*el Día de la Madre*
light blue	*azul claro*	the motorbike	*la moto*
light green	*verde claro*	the motorboat	*la lancha a motor*
a line	*una línea*	the motorcycle	*la motocicleta*
the lip	*el labio*	a mouse	*un ratón*
long	*largo*	the mouth	*la boca*
the long hair	*el cabello o pelo largo*	a movie	*una película*
lunch	*el almuerzo*	the movie theater	*el cine*
macrame	*el macramé*	Mr.	*Señor*
magic	*la magia*	Mrs.	*Señora*
a maid	*una empleada doméstica*	the muffin	*la magdalena*
the mail	*el correo*	the museum	*el museo*
a mail carrier	*un cartero, una cartera*	the mushroom	*el champiñón*
the mailbox	*el buzón*	the music	*la música*
the main course	*el plato principal*	the mustard	*la mostaza*
a man	*un hombre*	My address is . . .	*Mi dirección es . . .*
a manager	*un/una gerente*	my best friend	*mi mejor amigo*
a map	*un mapa*	My e-mail address is	*Mi dirección electrónica es*
March	*marzo*	My name is . . .	*Me llamo . . .*
the market	*el mercado*	My phone number is . . .	*Mi número de teléfono es . . .*
math	*matemáticas*	a napkin	*una servilleta*
May	*mayo*	narrow	*estrecho*
May I . . . ?	*¿Puedo . . . ?*	near	*cerca*
the mayonnaise	*la mayonesa*	neck	*el cuello*
Me too	*Yo también*	a necklace	*un collar*
meal	*la comida*	the needlepoint	*el medio punto*
mean	*cruel*	a neighbor	*un vecino, una vecina*
a mechanic	*un mecánico, una mecánica*	the nephew	*el sobrino*
medium (meats)	*término medio*	nervous	*inquieto, nervioso*
the menu	*el menú*	New Year's	*el Año Nuevo*
Mexican	*mexicano*	New Year's Eve	*el Fin de Año*
Mexico	*México*	next to	*junto a*

English	Spanish
nice	simpático
the niece	la sobrina
a nightgown	un camisón
nine	nueve
nineteen	diecinueve
ninety	noventa
no	no
north	norte
the nose	la nariz
a notebook	un cuaderno
Nothing (is new)	Nada, sin novedad
Nothing much	Nada de particular
November	noviembre
a nurse	un enfermero, una enfermera
a octagon	un octágono
October	octubre
offended	ofendido
an office	una oficina
the oil	el aceite
okay	de acuerdo
old	viejo
the olive	la aceituna
the omelet	el omelette
one	uno, una
one hundred	cien
one million	millón
one thousand	mil
a one-way ticket	un boleto sencillo
the onion	la cebolla
or	o
orange (color)	naranja
a orange (fruit)	una naranja
the orange juice	el jugo de naranja
outgoing	extrovertido
an oval	un óvalo
an oven	un horno
overseas	al extranjero
the painting	la pintura
some pajamas	unos piyamas
some panties	unas panties
some pants	unos pantalones
the paper	el papel

English	Spanish
a paper clip	un clip
pardon me	perdón, disculpe
the park	el parque
the parking space	el estacionamiento
a passenger	un pasajero
the passport	el pasaporte
the path	el camino
patient	paciente
the patio	el patio
a peach	un melocotón
peanuts	el maní
a pear	una pera
the peas	los guisantes
a pen	una pluma
a pencil	un lápiz
a pentagon	un pentágono
the pepper	la pimienta
Persian	persa
the pharmacy	la farmacia
the photography	la fotografía
the piano	el piano
the pie	la tarta, el pastel
a pilot	un/una piloto
the pinball machine	la máquina de pinball
a pineapple	una piña
ping pong	el tenis de mesa, ping-pong
pink	rosado
pistachios	los pistachos
the plane	el avión
a plane ticket	un boleto de avión
a plate	un plato
playful	juguetón
please	por favor
a plum	una ciruela
a plumber	un plomero, una plomera
poker	el póquer
Poland	Polonia
a police officer	un/una policía
the police station	la comisaría
Polish	el polaco
the pool (for swimming)	la piscina
pool (game)	el billar

English	Spanish
the porch	la terraza
the pork	el cerdo
Portuguese	el portugués
the post office	la oficina de correos
a poster	un cartel, un póster
a pot	una olla
the potato	la papa
the pottery	la alfarería
a printer	una impresora
Professor	profesor/profesora
Puerto Rican	puertorriqueño/a
purple	violeta
a purse	una cartera
a pyramid	una pirámide
quilting	hacer adredones
the rabbit	el conejo, la coneja
the radish	el rábano
a raincoat	un impermeable
rap	el rap
rare (meats)	término medio rojo
a raspberry	una frambuesa
a rat	una rata
reading	la lectura
a receptionist	un/una recepcionista
a rectangle	un rectángulo
red	rojo
red hair	el cabello o pelo rojo
a refrigerator	un refrigerador, una nevera
the restaurant	el restaurante
the rice	el arroz
the rice pudding	el arroz con leche
right	a la derecha
a ring	un anillo
the road	la calle
the roast beef	el rosbif
the rock and roll	el rock and roll
a romance movie	una película romántica
a romantic comedy	una comedia romántica
the room	el cuarto, la pieza
a round trip ticket	un boleto de ida y vuelta
a rubber band	una banda elástica
the rubber stamps	los sellos de goma

English	Spanish
a rug	un tapete
rugby	el rugby
a ruler	una regla
rummy	el rummy
running	correr
Russia	Rusia
Russian	ruso
the RV	la caravana
sad	triste
the sailboat	el barco de vela
sailing	la navegación a vela
the salad	la ensalada
the salt	la sal
same here	igualmente
some sandals	unas sandalias
the sandbox	el cajón de arena
the sandwich	el bocadillo, el sándwich
Saturday	sábado
a saucer	un platillo
the sausage	la salchicha
the saxophone	el saxofón
a scarf	una bufanda
a school	una escuela
science	la ciencia
the scissors	las tijeras
the scooter	el scooter, el ciclomotor
the scrapbook	el álbum de recortes
a screen door	una puerta mosquitera
the sculpture	la escultura
the seafood	los mariscos
a search engine	un motor de búsqueda
a secretary	un secretario, una secretaria
the security check	el control de seguridad
See you later	Hasta luego, Hasta pronto, Hasta la vista
See you next week	Hasta la semana próxima
See you tomorrow	Hasta mañana
September	septiembre
serious	serio
seven	siete
seventeen	diecisiete
seventy	setenta

English	Spanish	English	Spanish
sewing	la costura	south	sur
a shirt	una camisa	spades	las picas
a shoes	unos zapatos	Spain	España
short	bajo/a	Spaniard	el español, la española
short hair	el cabello o pelo corto	Spanish	español
the shorts	los pantalones cortos	a spatula	una espátula
the shoulder	el hombro	the spell checker	el corrector ortográfico
a shower	una ducha	the spelling	la ortografía
a shuttle	un servicio de autobús	a sphere	una esfera
shy	tímido/a	the spinach	las espinacas
sick	enfermo/a	a spoon	una cuchara
the sidewalk	la acera	a sports jacket	una chaqueta sport
a sink (in kitchen)	un fregadero	the spring	la primavera
a sink (in bathroom)	un lavamanos	a square	un cuadrado
the sister	la hermana	the stairway	la escalera
a sitcom	una comedia de situación	a staple	una grapa
six	seis	a stapler	una grapadora
sixteen	dieciséis	a star	una estrella
sixty	sesenta	the steak	el bistec
the skateboard	el monopatín	a stereo	un estéreo
the skateboarding	el monopatinaje	the stomach	el estómago
the skates	los patines	a stove	una estufa, una cocina
the skating	el patinaje	straight ahead	hacia adelante
skiing	esquiar	straight hair	el cabello o pelo liso
a skirt	una falda	a strawberry	una fresa
the slide	el tobogán	strong	fuerte
some slippers	unas pantuflas	a student	un/una estudiante
small	pequeño/a	a student desk	un pupitre
smart	inteligente	studious	estudioso/a
the smoothie	el licuado (de frutas)	the study	el despacho
a snake	una serpiente	stupid	estúpido/a
some sneakers	unos tenis	the subway	el metro
snobbish	presumido	the sugar	el azúcar
a soap opera	una telenovela	a suit	un traje
soccer	el fútbol	summer	el verano
social studies	los estudios sociales	Sunday	domingo
some socks	unos calcetines	some sunglasses	unas gafas de sol
the soda/pop	el refresco	the supermarket	el supermercado
the software	el software	a sweater	un suéter
solitaire	el solitario	swimming	la natación
the son	el hijo	the swing	el columpio
the soup	la sopa	Swiss	suizo

English	Spanish
Switzerland	Suiza
a table	una mesa
tall	alto/a
tanned	bronceado/a
the tap dance	el tap
the tape	la cinta adhesiva
a tarantula	una tarántula
the taxi	el taxi
the tea	el té
a teacher	un profesor, una profesora
a teenager	un/una joven
a telephone	un teléfono
a television set	un televisor
ten	diez
tennis	el tenis
the terminal	la terminal
a test	un examen
thank you	gracias
Thank you so much!	¡Cuánto se (te) lo agradezco!
thank you very much	muchas gracias
the theater	el teatro
thin	delgado
thirteen	trece
thirty	treinta
This is . . .	Este es . . .
three	tres
thumb	el pulgar
Thursday	jueves
a tie	una corbata
some tights	unas pantimedias
tiny	pequeñito
the tip	la propina
tip included	servicio incluido
tired	cansado
to be hungry	tener hambre
to be thirsty	tener sed
to board	embarcar
to brush (hair, teeth)	cepillarse
to buy a ticket	comprar un boleto
to comb (hair)	peinarse
to cook	cocinar
to do laundry	lavar la ropa

English	Spanish
to do the dishes	lavar los platos
to do the shopping	hacer las compras
to drink	beber
to eat	comer
to fall asleep	dormirse
to get dressed	vestirse
to get ready	arreglarse
to get tired	cansarse
to get up	levantarse
to go to bed	acostarse
to land	aterrizar
to make a reservation	hacer una reservación
to make the bed	hacer la cama
to mop the floor	fregar el piso
to mow the lawn	cortar el césped
to print	imprimir
to put on clothes	ponerse
to put on makeup	maquillarse, pintarse
to put the house in order	arreglar la casa
to read	leer
to save	archivar
to shave	afeitarse
to straighten up	poner en orden
to sweep the floor	barrer el piso
to take a bath	bañarse
to take a shower	ducharse
to take off	despegar
to take off clothes	quitarse
to take out the garbage	sacar la basura
the tuna	el atún
to type	escribir a máquina
to vacuum	pasar la aspiradora
to wake up	despertarse
to wash (up)	lavarse
to write	escribir
to write in cursive	escribir en cursiva
the toast	la tostada
toe	el dedo del pie
the tomato	el tomate
the tooth	el diente
the tornado	un tornado
the trail	el sendero

English	Spanish
the train	el tren
the tree	el árbol
a triangle	un triángulo
the tricycle	el triciclo
the truck	el camión
the trumpet	la trompeta
a T-shirt	una camiseta
Tuesday	martes
the turkey	el pavo
a turtle	una tortuga
a TV show	un programa de televisión
a TV station	una cadena de televisión
twelve	doce
twenty	veinte
two	dos
a typewriter	una máquina de escribir
ugly	feo/a
the uncle	el tío
an undershirt	una camiseta
the underwear	la ropa interior
United States	Estados Unidos
up	arriba
Valentine's Day	el Día de San Valentín
the van	la camioneta
the vanilla	la vainilla
the veal	la ternera
a videogame	un videojuego
Vietnamese	vietnamita
the violin	el violín
a visa	un visado
volleyball	el voleibol
a waiter, waitress	un camarero, una camarera
walking	a pie
a wall	una pared
a wallet	una billetera
the walnuts	las nueces
a washer	una lavadora
a watch	un reloj
the water	el agua
the wavy hair	el cabello o pelo ondulado
weak	débil
the weaving	el tejido

English	Spanish
a web page	una página web
a website	un sitio web
Wednesday	miércoles
well done (meats)	muy cocida
west	oeste
what	qué
What does mean?	¿Qué quiere decir ?
What's new?	¿Qué hay de nuevo?
What's your name?	¿Cómo te llamas?
when?	¿cuándo?
where?	¿dónde?
Where are you from?	¿De dónde eres?
Where are you going?	¿Adónde vas?
Where do you live?	¿Dónde vives?
Where is the . . . ?	¿Dónde está . . . ?
a whisk	un batidor
white	blanco/a
who	quién
Who are you?	¿Quién eres?
why	por qué
wide	ancho/a
wife	la esposa
a window	una ventana
wine	el vino
the winter	el invierno
a woman	una mujer
a wooden spoon	una cuchara de madera
the woods	el bosque
woodworking	la ebanistería
a word processor	un procesador de textos
wrestling	la lucha
the wrist	la muñeca
a writer	un escritor, una escritora
writing	la escritura
the yard	el jardín
yellow	amarillo
yes	sí
the yogurt	el yogur
young	joven
you're welcome	de nada
zero	cero

Fun Books and Websites

The Everything® Kids' Learning Spanish Book, 2nd Edition helps you to start learning Spanish, but there are a lot of other great books and websites that can help you learn and practice even more.

Books

The Everything® Kids' First Spanish Puzzle and Activity Book, by Laura K. Lawless and Beth L. Blair
> **A whole book of Spanish puzzles and activities to help you have fun while you practice your Spanish.**

Berlitz Kid's Spanish Picture Dictionary, by Berlitz International
> **See a picture of every word you look up.**

Beth Manners's Fun Spanish for Kids
> **A book and CD with Spanish stories, songs, and vocabulary for kids.**

Las puertas retorcidas, The Scariest Way in the World to Learn Spanish!, by Dr. Kathie Dior
> **Learn Spanish while reading and listening to a scary story about a house with twisted doors!**
> *www.home.thetwisteddoors.com*

Learn Spanish Together, by Marie-Clair Antoine
> **Activities, songs, and stickers make it fun to study Spanish.**

Speak Spanish with Dora and Diego, by Pimsleur
> **This book was designed for children ages two to six. Contains stories with vocabulary about family, breakfast, at school and at night. Includes two CDs and two books.**

Play and Learn Spanish, by Ana Lomba and Marcela Summerville, McGraw-Hill
> **For ages four to eight. It is a combination of hard copy book and a CD. The teaching is done using games, songs and activities with key-word illustrations to memorize words and phrases. The activities include daily routines like cooking, driving, and going shopping.**

Websites

Spanish for Children
> **Learn the alphabet, colors, and more with this interactive website.**
> *www.angelfire.com/de/cuento/color/inicial0.html*

StoryPlace
> **An online library for kids, with all kinds of stories and activities.**
> *www.storyplace.org/sp/storyplace.asp*

Viva Spanish
> **Lessons and practice on all kinds of useful Spanish vocabulary.**
> *www.vivaspanish.org*

A Parent-Teacher Guide

The purpose of this guide is to allow parents and teachers to help students with the subjects in each chapter of this book as well as to make the study time interesting, enjoyable and fun.

In order to keep the attention of younger students, it is important that you participate with them in activities for listening, speaking, and writing. This will make the kids feel that you are also part of the learning experience and will make them feel more inclined to go through the process.

You may want to consider making flashcards for the vocabulary so the student memorizes the words faster and in an organized way.

There are some words in Spanish that are said in different ways depending on the country. This book uses the most common ones and those that are going to be understood in most countries. If you go to a country that has a different name for a word, you can always learn that word there, and then you will have two words instead of one.

Here are some ideas on how to practice the material in this book lesson by lesson:

Chapter 1

- Practice the alphabet singing in a similar way you sing the English alphabet going from A to G, H to M, N to Q, R to V and W to Z.
- Review the numbers using groups of items of the same kind, such as beans for example. Work with numbers 1 to 10 several times and then 20 to 30, 30 to 40, and so on. After several repetitions for each group, you can add and remove some of the items so they can go back and forth and learn the numbers in a different order.
- Practice with feminine and masculine words as well as singular and plural. Most of the time feminine words end in *a* and masculine ones end in *o*. You can say for example *el padre* and the student will say *los padres* and vice versa.
- After the student has learned the conjugations, you say the part in English and ask the student to say the same thing in Spanish. For example: I speak—*Yo hablo.*

Do not worry that much about grammar details. You can always go back and refine some things. At this point what really matters is to learn the main components of the language.

Chapter 2

In this chapter the student will be learning some important phrases. After learning them you can do the following:

- Prepare some role-plays in which you will be asking the questions or giving the answers.
- If you are helping two or more students, you can make it fun by preparing a conversation for them using the phrases in this chapter.
- Give the students names in Spanish and change the names several times.

Chapter 3

Here you can continue to work with feminine, masculine, singular, and plural words.

- Give the student some drills in which he or she learns how to make the changes without thinking too much on how to do it. Retroactive learning is very beneficial.
- Remember to work with the pronouns *el*, *la*, *un*, and *unos*.

- Practice with the student describing himself and his friends. You can say something like "You have blond hair"—"*Tú tienes cabello rubio*" or "Sara has brown eyes"—"*Sara tiene ojos castaños.*"
- You can also practice describing personalities: "Brandon is kind"—"*Brandon es amable,*" "Kathy is studious"—"*Kathy es estudiosa*" and so on.
- You can also make some other combinations like: "You have dark hair and you are nice"—"*Tú tienes cabello oscuro y tú eres simpático.*"
- Remember that to describe feelings you need to use *estar* instead of *ser*. You can say something like "You are happy"—"*Tú estás feliz.*" Describe the student's friends using the feeling words in this chapter.

Chapter 4

To this point you already have a good idea on how to practice with the students using the subjects and vocabulary in this book. Here are some other ideas:

- When practicing the vocabulary, make it fun and loud. Ask the student to open her mouth wide and imagine the object. For example, if you say *la bicicleta*, say it loud and imagine a bicycle. You can also show a bicycle to the student so he can associate the word with the object.
- Talk with the student about her next vacation trip and asked her how she is going to go to that place—*en automóvil, en tren, en avión,* etc.
- After learning the shapes taught in this chapter ask the student to make a drawing using x amount of *cuadrados* with y amount of *triángulos* and so on. This way they can practice the numbers and also apply the vocabulary learned in this chapter.

Chapter 5

You can have a lot of fun in this chapter. Most of the vocabulary learned here is of things you have around the house so you have a lot of opportunity to practice it.

- Have the student learn the vocabulary thematically. For example, take him to the rooms around the house and show him what each word is, the balcony, the dining room, and so on. Say the word in Spanish with him. Have him work with the flashcards if you have them available. Again, the best way to learn the vocabulary is using flashcards.
- In the same way, practice with the student with the rest of the words in this chapter. If the kid is at an age in which she knows how to write it is important that you give her writing exercises. You can use the phrase "You need to . . . ." It means "*Tú necesitas . . . .*" You can write for example: "You need to make the bed"—"*Tú necesitas hacer la cama,*" and so on.

Chapter 6

You have finished with half of the lessons and your student has learned a lot of words and phrases already. You have enough materials to make things even more interesting.

- After you have worked with the words from this chapter, take some words and phrases from Chapters 1 to 5 and mix them around in conversation and writing.
- You can say something like "Where are the scissors?" "*¿Dónde están las tijeras?*" and the student will answer "The scissors are on the desk"—"*Las tijeras están en el escritorio.*" You need to be creative on how to mix the different phrases and vocabulary taught in previous chapters so your students are successful with their Spanish.
- To have the students work on their writing you can prepare some fill in the blanks exercises with phrases like

   "Where is/are _____"
   "I want _____ " "
   I have _____ " etc.

Chapter 7

This is a great lesson to continue with the review of numbers.

- Make your own clock with a piece of cardboard or buy one at a school supply store. Move the clock needles and ask the student to say the hour in Spanish. If it is your child and you are ready to buy him a watch, you can motivate him by saying that he will have a watch once he knows how to say the time in English and Spanish.

- Practice the dates asking the student to say in Spanish her birthday and her friends' birthdays. Also, ask what she is going to do on her birthday.

Chapter 8

Here is a great opportunity to prepare a healthy menu with the child.

- While you are learning the vocabulary ask the student what foods he likes. You can ask "What do you like?"—"*¿Qué te gusta?*" Once he has picked some foods, you can prepare a menu in Spanish including those foods.
- Take the student to the supermarket and ask her to say the names of the different foods in Spanish. Remember to take the vocabulary list with you in case she forgets a word.
- Because food is always around, you can ask the student once in a while for the name of different foods he has learned. This can be done even outside of your learning schedule.

Chapter 9

For this international chapter, have a globe or a map out to practice with the student.

- Show the student the country and ask her the name of the country, the nationality of the people from that country, and the language spoken in that country. If you prefer you can practice these words separately. Practice first the countries names, then the nationalities, and finally the languages. Once the student knows them well, you can challenge her with country, nationality, and language.

- Practice with the student, asking him what he wants to be when he grows up. The way to ask the question is "*¿Qué quieres ser cuando seas grande?*" The student will answer "I want to be a pilot/a doctor/a cook . . ."—"*Quiero ser un piloto/una doctora/un cocinero . . . .*"

Chapter 10

In this chapter the student learns how to do all those fun things in Spanish. There are a lot of ways in which you will be able to practice with the student.

- Ask the student what sports he likes to play and what others he likes to watch. You can ask him "*¿Qué deportes te gusta jugar?*" and "*¿Qué deportes te gusta mirar?*"
- Do the same thing with board games. If you are playing cards you can also ask the student to name the different suits and face cards.
- The main phrases you are going to need to ask the student what sport, activity, movie, and so on, he likes are:

Do you like _____?

¿Te gusta _____?

What is your favorite _____?

¿Cuál es tu _____ favorito/favorita?

Congratulations! You have followed the suggestions in this guide and you can see the results in your student's progress. Remember that a second language is something that will be forgotten if not used. Go back once in a while and review with the student the vocabulary and phrases to make sure that they stay in the student's long-term memory.

Puzzle Answers

page 3 • Alphabet Code

What kind of insect does well in school?

AH
A

ESeh PEH EH ELeh ELeh EE ENeh HEH
S P E L L I N G

BEH EH EH
B E E

page 6 • Jumping Numbers

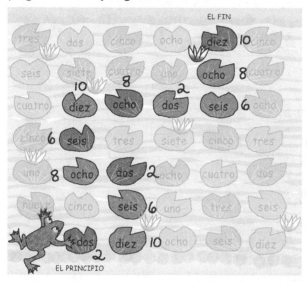

page 13 • Hey You!

page 19 • Questions, Questions

page 22 • Night and Day

page 26 • Hi, Llama!

page 39 • **Face to Face**

"Yo" means "I."

I see <u>with</u> my <u>eyes</u>.
Yo veo <u>con</u> mis <u>ojos</u>.

I smell <u>with</u> my <u>nose</u>.
Yo huelo <u>con</u> mi <u>nariz</u>.

I hear <u>with</u> my <u>ears</u>.
Yo oigo <u>con</u> mis <u>orejas</u>.

I eat <u>with</u> my <u>mouth</u>.
Yo como <u>con</u> mi <u>boca</u>.

I taste <u>with</u> my <u>tongue</u>.
Yo pruebo <u>con</u> mi <u>lengua</u>.

page 49 • **Gotta Go!**

~~UNO~~	DÓNDE	~~EL HIJO~~
ESTÁ	~~PAPÁ~~	~~OCHO~~
~~ROJO~~	EL	~~AZUL~~
~~LA TÍA~~	~~SEIS~~	BAÑO
POR	~~VERDE~~	FAVOR

¿DÓNDE ESTÁ EL
BAÑO, POR FAVOR?

page 58 • **My Room**

UNA CAMA
(a bed)

page 44 • **All Around Town**

1. The library
2. The school
3. The park
4. The post office
5. The supermarket

page 69 • **Reading List**

What do all students need to read?

U — letter right after T
N — letter just before O

U — letter between K and M
L — the ninth letter
I — the second letter
B — the second letter after P
R — letter right after N
O —

page 72 •
Dressed for Work

EL CASCO
EL ABRIGO
LOS GUANTES
LOS PANTALONES
LAS BOTAS

EL PERRO

Puzzle Answers

page 84 • Nice Party

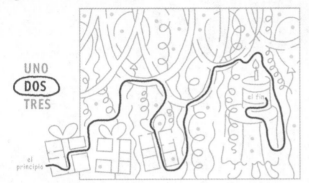

page 90 • Let's Eat Lunch!

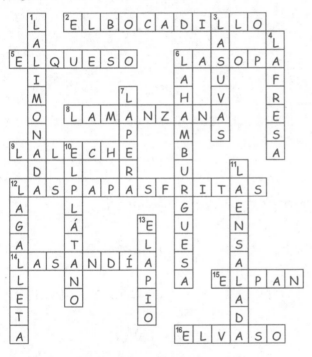

page 95 • Hidden Foods

1. Food fight! Splat art! Annoy mom!
2. In a tunnel, a car never goes fast.
3. A morsel, Pa. Not a lot!
4. I eat food of land and sea.
5. I will fill a salad bowl.

page 109 • I Win!

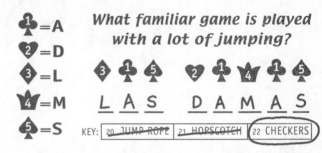

What familiar game is played with a lot of jumping?

L A S   D A M A S

KEY: 20 JUMP ROPE | 21 HOPSCOTCH | 22 CHECKERS

♣ = A
♦ = D
♥ = L
♠ = M
♣ = S

page 115 • Nifty Knitter

WORD LIST
3 el corazón *heart*
1 el pollo *chicken*
6 el gusano *worm*
2 el diamante *diamond*
4 la llave *key*
5 la cometa *kite*